The Second Message of Islam

Contemporary Issues in the Middle East

Ustadh Mahmoud at home in Omdurman, Sudan, in 1982.
Photo by Omar Stefanoff.

The Second Message of Islam

Mahmoud Mohamed Taha

Translation and Introduction by

Abdullahi Ahmed An-Na'im

Syracuse University Press

94 93 92 91 90 89 8 87 6 5 4 3 2 1

The paper used in this publication meets the minimum requirements of American National Standard for Information Sciences—Permanence of Paper for Printed Library Materials, ANSI Z39.48-1984. ∞

Library of Congress Cataloging-in-Publication Data

Tāhā, Mahmūd Muhammad.
  The second message of Islam.

  (Contemporary issues in the Middle East)
  Translation of: al-Risālah al-thāniyah min al-Islām.
  Includes index.
  1. Islam—20th century. 2. Islam—Doctrines.
I. Title. II. Series.
BP163.T28513 1987   297'.2   87-428
ISBN 0-8156-2407-7 (alk. paper)

To humanity!
Good tidings . . . and greetings.
Good tidings it is that God has in store for us such perfection of intellectual and emotional life as no eye has ever seen, no ear has ever heard, and has never occurred to any human being.

Greetings to Man, as he stirs today in the womb of parturient humanity, and the dawn of birth breaks.

Mahmoud Mohamed Taha

Omdurman, Sudan
January 1967

Abdullahi Ahmed An-Na'im graduated in law from the University of Khartoum. He obtained an LL.B. degree from Cambridge University, and a Ph.D. in law from the University of Edinburgh. Dr. An-Na'im was Rockefeller Fellow in Human Rights at Columbia University, 1981–82. In 1983–84 he was held without trial during the mass detention of members of the Republican Brothers related in this book. Dr. An-Na'im teaches law at the University of Khartoum. During 1985–87 he was Visiting Professor of Law at UCLA.

Contents

The Second Message of Islam

Translator's Introduction

The Second Message of Islam is the main text of the movement started and led by *Ustadh* (revered teacher) Mahmoud Mohamed Taha, the late Sudanese Muslim reformer who was executed by former President Numeiri of Sudan on January 18, 1985. Although Ustadh Mahmoud asked me to translate this book in 1980, and I finished the first complete draft in April 1982, it was only after the execution of Ustadh Mahmoud in January 1985, and the overthrow of President Numeiri in April of the same year, that I was able to resume my effort to have the translation revised and finalized for publication. It is now clear to me that the delay was fortunate in that it enabled me to reflect in this introduction on the significance of the life and work of Ustadh Mahmoud in light of the manner and circumstances of his death and other recent developments not only in Sudan but also in other parts of the Muslim world. Although originating in Sudan, where he lived all his life and did all his religious and intellectual work, his thought seems destined to have lasting and far-reaching consequences throughout the Muslim world. It is even possible that eventually it may influence the course of international events.

Some of the implications of this book and other aspects of the life and work of Ustadh Mahmoud will be outlined below. One cannot exaggerate the importance of his humane and liberating understanding of Islam as an alternative to the cruel and oppressive interpretation underlying recent events in Iran, Pakistan, and Sudan, and the equally negative traditionalist view prevailing in Saudi Arabia and other parts of the Muslim world. He has succeeded in convincing many Muslims that there is much more to Islam than senseless harsh penalties and segregation and discrimination against women and non-Muslims. In light of his life and work, Islam can offer its adherents an intelligent, dynamic world view capable of accommodating and promoting the full moral, intellectual, and artistic vitality of modern society.

After a brief biographical note on Ustadh Mahmoud Mohamed Taha, and a general survey of his social and political reform movement in Sudan, this introduction will suggest the broader implications of *The Second Message of Islam*, in order to show its significance not only to Muslims all over the world, but also to the ongoing global debate over the moral and ideological issues it discusses. It may then be helpful to consider the prospects for a wide-scale implementation of this revolutionary Muslim ideology. At the end of this introduction, a few remarks will be made on the style and methodology of this translation.

THE MAN AND HIS MOVEMENT

Mahmoud Mohamed Taha was born in either 1909 or 1911 in Rufa'h, a small town on the east bank of the Blue Nile of central Sudan.[1] His mother died around 1915, and his father followed her around 1920, leaving their children to be brought up by the extended family. Mahmoud was the only one of the children to complete the extremely competitive educational system of the time. He graduated from the engineering school of Gordon Memorial College, now the University of Khartoum, in 1936. Following a short period of service with Sudan Railways, he resigned and went into private practice in the early 1940s.

As an active participant in the nationalist struggle for independence from the beginning of the movement in the late 1930s, Ustadh Mahmoud was dissatisfied with the performance of the educated elite in that struggle. He criticized them for submitting their expertise to the sectarian traditional religious leaders who commanded wide popular support in the country as a whole. The available political parties were also unacceptable to him as they seemed to be willing to accept the patronage of the colonial powers, thereby compromising their commitment to full independence and the establishment of a Sudanese republic.[2] Ustadh Mah-

---

1. I have personally heard this formulation of the estimated date of his birth from *Ustadh* Mahmoud himself. No formal birth records were kept in that part of the country at the time.

2. Sudan was ruled as an Anglo-Egyptian condominium from 1898 until full independence was achieved in January 1, 1956. Rivalry between the dominant partner, Britain, and the weaker partner, Egypt, which happened to be traditionally more influential in the

moud and other intellectuals who agreed with his criticism formed the Republican Party in October of 1945. The organization's first publication and subsequent pamphlets and leaflets reflected a strong modernist Islamic orientation which, at the time, was not yet fully developed.

The party's policy of direct and open confrontation with the colonial authorities led to the arrest and subsequent imprisonment of Ustadh Mahmoud and several of his colleagues in 1946. Ustadh Mahmoud was sentenced to prison for a year when he refused to abstain from political activity against the colonial government. In response to the mounting protest orchestrated by the Republican Party, he was "pardoned" by the British Governor-General and released after fifty days in prison. He did not stay free for long, however. In the same year he was arrested, tried, and sentenced to two years' imprisonment for his role in what came to be known as the Rufa'h incident. In order to convey the significance of that incident in terms of the substance of Ustadh Mahmoud's thought and his method of political action, I will briefly describe the background of his second conviction and prison sentence in 1946.

In that year the colonial government of Sudan added section 284A to the Sudan Penal Code forbidding the practice of a severe type of female circumcision known as Pharaonic circumcision (removing all the external genital organs of girls). While vigorously opposed to the practice itself, the Republican Party resisted the introduction of penal measures as not only ineffective, but actually counter-productive. The organization maintained that such deep-rooted social customs could not be changed by imposing criminal sanction; instead, such laws might actually reinforce what was still regarded as a socially desirable practice, despite the threat of prosecution.[3] They also criticized the high-handed methods and arrogant attitudes of the colonial administration, which they accused of bad faith and of using the issue to create negative external publicity against Sudan as one way of resisting Sudanese demands for independence. The Republicans said that if the government was genuinely concerned with

---

region, was reflected in the Sudanese national struggle for independence, as the ruling powers competed in conferring patronage on the emerging Sudanese political organizations.

3. This criticism may now be vindicated by the fact that despite the existence of the penal provision, the practice of Pharaonic circumcision continues up to the present time, except in those parts of the country where education and general enlightenment have succeeded in changing social attitudes in this regard. Moreover, the threat of prosecution may force the practice to be secret, thereby increasing its medical and psychological dangers.

improving general health conditions and the welfare of Sudanese women, it should work to educate the female population in general, so that unhealthy and harmful practices, including female circumcision, might be voluntarily and intelligently abandoned.

In accordance with this position, and in order to use the incident in mobilizing nationalist public opinion against the colonial administration, the Republicans set out to resist the prosecution of a woman in Rufa'h for subjecting her own daughter to this prohibited form of female circumcision. Following speeches on the issue at a Friday prayer meeting in the main mosque of the town,[4] Ustadh Mahmoud led thousands of men across the Blue Nile into the administrative center of the district, Hassaheissa, and succeeded in freeing the accused woman on the spot. As a result, he and several other leaders of the small revolt were subsequently arrested, tried, and sentenced to prison. As the leader of the revolt, Ustadh Mahmoud received the harshest sentence: two years' imprisonment.

It was during this second term of imprisonment, and the subsequent period of self-imposed religious seclusion (khalwah) in his home town of Rufa'h, that Ustadh Mahmoud undertook the rigorous program of prayer, fasting, and meditation that led to his insights into the meaning of the Qur'an and the role of Islamic law. These he subsequently articulated as the "second message" of Islam.

Throughout his life Ustadh Mahmoud emphasized that his vision of the future of Islam was God-given and not the result of purely rational secular thinking. He was always careful to state clearly, however, that he had not received any fresh revelation, as he shared the common Muslim belief that all heavenly revelation ended with the Prophet Mohamed. Nevertheless, he maintained that since the Qur'an is the literal word of God, human beings can receive an enlightened understanding of the word and learn from God directly through His word as revealed to the Prophet. The only limitation on human powers of comprehension of the word of God, and the only cause of human failure to learn what He is teaching them all the time, are the impurities they accumulate in their impious and unreflective daily existence. By rigorously and intelligently pursuing reflective worship and other practices of the Prophet Mohamed, argued Ustadh Mahmoud, human beings could sharpen their senses and develop their faculties, thereby becoming ready to appreciate and understand what God teaches through the Qur'an. In support of this argument, he often

4. Friday noon prayer is the formal weekly congregational prayer for Muslims.

cited verse 282 of chapter 2 of the Qur'an, which states that God teaches the one who is pious and fearful of God. He also cited the *Sunnah*, or tradition of the Prophet, that states that the person who acts in accordance with what he or she knows shall be granted by God knowledge of that which he or she does not know.[5]

By the end of his period of seclusion in October 1951, Ustadh Mahmoud emerged with a comprehensive vision of what he later termed the second message of Islam. He continued to preach it, through lectures, newspaper articles, and books, until his death in January 1985. The Republican Party was transformed in the early 1950s from a political party in the usual sense of the term into an organization for the propagation of this vision. Those members of the organization who wanted to pursue a more secular political role broke away and joined other political parties. For those who remained with the party, the organization became a spiritual environment under the guidance of Ustadh Mahmoud.

After a short period of service with the Water and Electricity Company in Khartoum, Ustadh Mahmoud resumed his private practice as an engineer in the mid 1950s. He continued to write, lecture, and debate his views through every available venue until the early 1970s, when the Numeiri regime banned his public lectures.[6] For most of the remaining years of his life, he confined himself to guiding the activities of the organization by then known as the Republican Brothers, which included a growing number of women members.[7] Both male and female members of the organization continued to propagate the Second Message of Islam despite harassment by some officials and members of the security forces.

Since it was crucial to Ustadh Mahmoud that he should practice what he preached, he tried to establish a community which applied, as far as possible, the main tenets of his vision of Islam. As a small community within Sudanese society, the Republicans were unable to implement the full scope of their beliefs in the Organization of the Sudanese state, but they strove to lead their personal lives and organize their own community

5. This is not of course a novel position within the Islamic tradition. Many leading *sufi* (mystic) religious leaders have maintained this position during lengthy, and often heated, debates with the traditional formalistic scholars of Islamic jurisprudence.

6. Ustadh Mahmoud was willing to defy the ban, but nobody was prepared to give him a platform or provide him with access to the media.

7. At one point the group debated changing its name to reflect its female membership and the real nature of the organization. They finally decided to keep the old name because it was already well established and known to the public as a religious intellectual movement of both men and women.

in accordance with those beliefs. In particular, the community largely succeeded in applying the principles of equality between men and women, without discrimination on grounds of sex. Women members participated fully in all the group's activities, and they were often leaders of activist groups on university campuses and in public parks and street corners—a highly controversial practice in the Sudanese patriarchal society. This was such a hallmark of the movement that when the leadership of the organization was detained without charge in mid-1983, four women were among their number.[8]

The group's practice in relation to contracting marriage is illustrative of the members' determination to implement their theory in light of prevailing social customs. Besides submitting to the most restrictive historical formulations of Islamic law, Shari'a, the marriage practices of the northern and central Sudan conformed to several restrictive legal and social norms. Although the Hanafi school of Islamic jurisprudence applied by the Shari'a Family Law Courts of the Sudan permitted a husband to give his wife the right to divorce herself unilaterally, no use was made of this provision in actual practice.[9] Further, the Qur'anic principle of arbitration (tahkim) to settle family disputes, based on verse 35 of chapter 4 of the Qur'an, was not used. Instead, marital differences were routinely submitted to the formal courts, which were unsuitable for settling such delicate and personal issues with the sensitivity and candor of private arbitration. In the male-dominated and formalistic courts, women often suffered the indignity of public exposure of the most intimate details of their lives without obtaining effective redress for their grievances.

At the social level, moreover, marriage ceremonies were typically conducted with great extravagance, both in the payment of an exorbitant bride-price (mahr) and in the need to give expensive banquets and parties. As can be expected, such excessive costs placed heavy burdens on families and generally discouraged young couples from getting married. Furthermore, a high bride-price often had negative consequences on the matrimonial relationship itself.

In 1971 the Republicans adopted an integrated plan to resolve these legal and social problems of marriage. All Republican couples have been

8. Ustadh Mahmoud's only two daughters and one of his nieces were among the four women detainees.

9. Family and personal law matters for Muslims in the Sudan were always governed by Shari'a, even during the colonial Anglo-Egyptian administration of 1898–1956. Due to the Ottoman-Egyptian influence on the administration of justice, however, the official version of Shari'a applied by the courts was that of the Hanafi school of Islamic jurisprudence. (See generally C. D. Farran, *Matrimonial Laws of the Sudan* [London: Butterworth, 1963].)

conducting their marriages in full accordance with this plan since that time.[10] At the legal level, husbands have extended the right of divorce to their wives in the marriage contract itself. Previously married Republicans have added a similar stipulation to their preexisting contracts. Binding arbitration clauses were also added to the marriage contracts. In this way, both husband and wife had the right to unilateral divorce, subject to the binding ruling of the arbiters of both parties. If either party should insist on a divorce, he or she would be entitled to obtain it, while remaining bound by the ruling of the arbiters on the financial and other consequences of the dissolution of marriage. Since each party had the right to appoint his or her own arbiter, a wife would be equally represented in the two-person panel that decided these matters.

Bride-price was kept to the absolute minimum required for the validity of the contract of marriage under Shari'a. One Sudanese pound was paid to comply with this formality. In due course, the Republicans hope to dispense with this formality, when Shari'a law is reformed to remove the requirement of *mahr* altogether. In the meantime, the drastic reduction of monetary *mahr* was designed to emphasize that no price is sufficient to purchase a wife, thereby signifying that marriage is an equal partnership. (This purpose would of course be better achieved if *mahr* were abolished altogether, but that is not possible under the present circumstances.)

At the social level, the Republicans dispensed with all wedding banquets and parties. Marriage contracts were concluded in a simple ceremony during which only soft drinks and dates were offered to the guests, in accordance with everyday Sudanese hospitality. Having attended the ceremony in everyday dress, the couple leave the scene as husband and wife to make their own independent choice of living arrangements.

In this way, the Republicans revolutionized marriage practices within the confines of Shari'a without offending the essence of prevailing social customs. This commitment to practice their theory while remaining sensitive to legal and social norms characterized the Republican approach to reform.

Ustadh Mahmoud's public lectures were banned beginning in 1973, and his disciples operated with some difficulty throughout most of Numeiri's rule. Although their activities were always within the law, their

10. Although the project was designed to be open to all Sudanese Muslims, since it is in full accord with Shari'a as recognized by the Sudanese courts, very few nonmembers have followed the Republican example.

views tended to arouse opposition from traditional and fundamentalist religious and political circles.[11] Their opponents succeeded at times in applying various administrative and executive mechanisms to obstruct or limit the effectiveness of the Republicans. Denied access to the media, which were all state-owned at that time, the Republicans had to prepare their own publications and seek unorthodox channels to reach the public. They had to resort, for example, to the use of street corners and public parks to address whoever was willing to stop and listen to what they had to say. The police often intervened to break up those spontaneous public meetings, charging the Republicans conducting the meetings with "breach of the peace" and "disturbance of public tranquility."[12] The Republicans' frequent protests against those infringements of their fundamental constitutional rights were futile. The harassment continued, culminating in the mass detentions of 1983 and the execution of Ustadh Mahmoud in 1985.

Despite these restrictions, the Republicans supported the regime of former President Numeiri throughout the 1970s and into the early 1980s. Their support was forthcoming as long as the regime maintained policies of national unity and refrained from applying Shari'a to the detriment of women and non-Muslim Sudanese. The Republicans also believed that the regime of President Numeiri was preferable to the only available alternative, a sectarian and "fundamentalist" civilian dictatorship. Only after Shari'a was imposed by presidential decrees beginning in August of 1983, thereby undermining national unity between the Muslim north and non-Muslim south and leading to harsh and repressive policies in the country as a whole, did the Republicans declare their opposition. In other words, their opposition was prompted by the change in the nature and policies of the regime rather than the 1983 detention of the group's leadership as such. Ustadh Mahmoud himself had previously been detained together with eight leaders of the group, for one month in 1977 without charge. He had also personally suffered what was in effect a total

11. The term "Muslim fundamentalist" is currently popularly used to refer to those who demand the immediate implementation of historical Islamic Shari'a law. Otherwise, the Republicans would claim to be fundamentalist in the sense of advocating a return to the fundamental sources of Islam to develop a modern version of Islamic law.

12. As an attorney, I have often acted as defense counsel for Republicans facing such charges, with acquittal being the invariable result, since no offense was committed in the first place. It seems that the object of the police was to disrupt the meetings and discourage the participants without any serious desire to prosecute, because the policeman making the arrest and filing the initial complaint usually failed to appear and pursue the prosecution. Cases were accordingly dismissed for that reason.

ban on his public activities since 1973. The group endured those restrictions and harassment for over ten years without opposing the regime of former President Numeiri.

The immediate or apparent cause of the detention in mid 1983 was a pamphlet issued by the Republicans criticizing what they perceived to be the failure of the chief of state security, who also happened to be the first vice-president of the republic, to check Muslim fundamentalists' incitement of religious hatred and abetment of violence against the Republicans and against non-Muslim Sudanese.[13] In hindsight, however, and in the light of subsequent developments, it would seem that at least the continuation of the leaders' detention, if not the initial sweeping detention order, was motivated by other considerations. A few weeks after their detention, President Numeiri announced his intention to impose Shari'a law. If the Republicans were free, it must have been thought, they would actively oppose that policy, because it contravened their long-held position that there must be radical reform of Shari'a prior to its modern implementation. When that policy materialized in a series of enactments starting in August 1983,[14] the Republicans started an opposition campaign with their leadership still in detention. Despite their active opposition to President Numeiri's policy of imposed Islamization, or perhaps because of that opposition, the Republicans were all released on December 19, 1984, after approximately nineteen months in detention without charge.[15] Whether it occurred in response to mounting international pressure protesting the detention of the group,[16] or as a deliberate

13. The pamphlet cited in particular the activities of a certain Egyptian fundamentalist operating in Khartoum at the time. The same man, *Shiekh* al-Muti'y, alleged the pamphlet, was responsible for inciting religious violence between Muslims and Christians in Cairo in 1981.

14. President Numeiri enacted the first eight "Islamic" statutes by presidential decree in August and September of 1983. The People's Assembly was reconvened in November, whereupon it proceeded to approve the president's decrees during its first week of business. The President continued to enact other major "Islamic" laws, such as the *Zakah* and Taxation Act and the Civil Transactions Act, by presidential decree while the Assembly was in session. The Republicans issued their first pamphlet in opposition to those enactments in March 1984, when the courts began to implement the new Acts.

15. Most of the Republican detainees were not even interviewed by any official or security officer throughout that period. I speak here from personal experience, having been the victim of such detention without charge or even an interview between May 17, 1983 and December 19, 1984. As we were all held in the same prison in Khartoum North, I know that this was the case with the majority of Republican detainees.

16. All the Republican detainees were adopted as prisoners of conscience by Amnesty International, which continued to demand their immediate release through its headquar-

trap to involve the Republicans in overt acts rendering them liable to prosecution under the new laws, the mass release on December 19, 1984, marked the beginning of the fatal sequence of events culminating in the execution of Ustadh Mahmoud four weeks later.

THE MURDER OF A PACIFIST

While aware that he and other Republican leaders had been released only to be pursued under the new laws, Ustadh Mahmoud immediately assumed responsibility for the campaign against President Numeiri's Islamization policy. Within one week of their release—on December 25, 1984—the first leaflet was published demanding repeal of the new laws and a guarantee of democratic civil liberties under which to debate the principles and process of Islamization. To assist the reader in assessing some of the following criticisms of the trial and execution of Ustadh Mahmoud for publishing this leaflet, the full text of the leaflet is translated here:

In the name of God, the Beneficent, the Merciful

Either This or the Flood

And guard against a turmoil that will not befall the unfair ones alone, and know that God is severe in punishment." (Qur'an chapter 8, verse 25)

We, the Republicans, have dedicated our lives to the promotion and protection of two honorable objectives namely, Islam and the Sudan. To this end we have propagated Islam at the scientific level as capable of resolving the problems of modern life. We have also sought to safeguard the superior moral values and original ethics conferred by God upon this people [the Sudanese], thereby making them the appropriate transmitters of Islam to the whole of modern humanity, which has no salvation nor dignity except through this religion [Islam].

The September 1983 Laws [that is, the series of enactments purporting to impose Shari'a law in the Sudan] have distorted Islam in the

---

ters in London and various local chapters all over the world. Some friends of individual Republicans, such as Professor William Alford of the UCLA School of Law and Mr. Kenneth Brecher, were able to involve leading personalities in a letter-writing campaign seeking the release of the Republicans in the Sudan.

eyes of intelligent members of our people and in the eyes of the world, and degraded the reputation of our country. These laws violate Shari'a and violate religion itself. They permit, for example, the amputation of the hand of one who steals public property, although according to Shari'a the appropriate penalty is the discretionary punishment (ta'zir) and not the specific (hadd) penalty for theft, because of the doubt (shubha) raised by the participation of the accused in the ownership of such [public] property. These unfair laws have added imprisonment and fine to the specified (hadd) penalties in contravention of the provisions of Shari'a and their rationale. They have also humiliated and insulted the people [of this country] who have seen nothing of these laws except the sword and the whip, although they are a people worthy of all due respect and reverence. Moreover, the enforcement of the specified penalties [hudod and qassas] presupposes a degree of individual education and social justice which are lacking today.

These laws have jeopardized the unity of the country and divided the people in the north and south [of the country] by provoking religious sensitivity, which is one of the fundamental factors that has aggravated the southern problem [that is, conflict and civil war in the non-Muslim southern part of the country]. It is futile for anyone to claim that a Christian person is not adversely affected by the implementation of Shari'a. A Muslim under Shari'a is the guardian of a non-Muslim in accordance with the "verse of the sword" and the "verse of jiziah" [respectively calling the Muslims to use arms to spread Islam, and for the imposition of a humiliating poll tax on the subjugated Christians and Jews—verses 5 and 29 of chapter 9 of the Qur'an]. They do not have equal rights. It is not enough for a citizen today merely to enjoy freedom of worship. He is entitled to the full rights of a citizen in total equality with all other citizens. The rights of southern citizens in their country are not provided for in Shari'a but rather in Islam at the level of fundamental Qur'anic revelation, that is, the level of Sunnah. We therefore call for the following:

1. The repeal of the September 1983 laws because they distort Islam, humiliate the people, and jeopardize national unity.

2. The halting of bloodshed in the south and the implementation of a peaceful political solution instead of a military solution [to the civil war in the southern part of the country]. This is the national duty of the government as well as the armed southerners. There must be the brave admission that the South has a genuine problem and the serious attempt to resolve it.

3. We call for the provision of full opportunities for the enlightenment and education of this [Sudanese] people so as to revive Islam at the level of Sunnah [the fundamental Qur'an]. Our times call for Sunnah

not Shari'a [the distinction is explained in the text of this book]. The Prophet, peace be upon him, said: "Islam started as a stranger, and it shall return as a stranger in the same way it started . . . Blessed are the strangers . . . They [his companions] said: Who are the strangers, Oh, Messenger of God? He [the Prophet] replied: Those who revive my Sunnah after it has been abandoned."

This level of Islamic revival shall achieve pride and dignity for the people. In this level, too, lies the systematic solution for the southern problem as well as the northern problem [that is, the socioeconomic and political problems of the northern part of the country]. Religious fanaticism and backward religious ideology can achieve nothing for this [Sudanese] people except upheaval and civil war.

Here is our genuine and honest advice. We offer it on the occasion of the Christmas and Independence Day [December 25 and January 1, which is Sudan's Independence Day], and may God expedite its acceptance and safeguard the country against upheaval and preserve its independence, unity, and security.

25th December 1984   The Republicans
2 Rabi' Al-Thany 1405 A.H.   OMDURMAN

The initial police reaction to the leaflet was ambivalent, because of the recent mass release of the Republicans. Moreover, the mild language and content of the leaflet itself gave no cause for serious charges under existing laws. Some police districts arrested a few Republicans who were found distributing the leaflet and charged them with the minor offense of breach of the peace under section 127 of the penal code. In some cases, however, police officers actually intervened to instruct an arresting policeman to release a Republican because no offense was committed. [17]

It was at this point that the state minister for criminal affairs intervened and instructed public prosecutors in the three towns of Khartoum, Omdurman, and Khartoum North to press charges of sedition, undermining the constitution, inciting unlawful opposition to the government, and disturbing public tranquility under sections 96, 105 and 127A of the Penal

17. This survey of the sequence of events is based on my own personal follow-up of these cases as the Attorney for the Republicans and leading participant at all stages. In that capacity, I was able to see official correspondence, court records etc., and talk to ministers, public prosecutors, judges and police officers, some of whom were my colleagues or former students at the Faculty of Law, University of Khartoum and the Sudan Police Academy.

Code of 1983, as well as membership in an unlawful organization under section 20 of the State Security Act of 1973. With the charges thereby transformed into capital offenses, ten recently arrested Republicans were to remain in custody, as the new charges permitted no release on bail.

On Wednesday, January 2, 1985, the four Republicans who were arrested and charged in Omdurman central district were brought to trial before one of the special criminal courts established under the Judiciary Act of 1984.[18] The trial was adjourned, however, because the serious charges required the special sanction of the president of the republic.[19] On Saturday afternoon, January 5, Ustadh Mahmoud was arrested at his house in Omdurman and charged with the same combination of offenses. On Monday morning, January 7, Ustadh Mahmoud and the original four Republicans were brought to trial before the special criminal court after sanction for the trial was obtained from the president of the republic. It is important to note here that the president's sanction included the directive to add section 458(3) and the penal code to the charges. That section authorized the court to impose any *hadd* penalty, that is, specific penalty provided for by Shari'a, regardless of the lack of statutory penal provision. That section violated the express provisions of Article 70 of the 1973 Constitution, which was still in force at the time.[20] But because the five accused decided to boycott the trial proceedings because of their objections to the laws under which the court was constituted and purported to act, and also because of their objections to the calibre of the judges presiding in those courts, the unconstitutionality of charges under section 458(3) of the penal code was never discussed at any stage of the case.

18. Like all those special criminal courts established under the Judiciary Act of 1984, the court was manned by a single judge appointed by the President of the Republic under Section 32 of the Act which authorized such appointments irrespective of qualifications for appointment to judicial office required by the same Act. The judge conducting this particular trial which was to include Ustadh Mahmoud himself as we shall see, was Hassan Ibrahim al-Mahalawy, a fresh graduate who had less than three years of practical judicial experience.

19. Section 148 of the Code of Criminal Procedure of 1983, corresponding to section 131 of the old Code, required the special sanction of the President of the Republic for prosecutions under certain specified sections of the Penal Code and other penal enactments.

20. This section of the penal code had already been challenged by the Republicans in their constitutional suits of January 1984. Those suits were dismissed by the Supreme Court, which was reconstituted under the "Islamic" Judiciary Act of 1983. The court ruled that the Republicans who brought those constitutional challenges to the "Islamic" laws of 1983 lacked the personal interest necessary to give them legal standing to bring the suits.

In announcing his decision to boycott the proceedings, *Ustadh* Mahmoud improvised the following statement:

I have repeatedly declared my view that the September 1983 so-called Islamic laws violate Islamic Shari'a law and Islam itself. Moreover, these laws have distorted Islamic Shari'a law and Islam and made them repugnant. Furthermore, these laws were enacted and utilized to terrorize the people and humiliate them into submission. These laws also jeopardize the national unity of the country [by discriminating against non-Muslim citizens—about one third of the population]. These are [my] objections from the theoretical point of view.

At the practical level, the judges enforcing these laws lack the necessary technical qualifications. They have also morally failed to resist placing themselves under the control of the executive authorities which exploited them in violating the rights of citizens, humiliating the people, distorting Islam, insulting intellect and intellectuals, and humiliating political opponents.

For all these reasons, I am not prepared to cooperate with any court that has betrayed the independence of the judiciary and allowed itself to be a tool for humiliating the people, insulting free thought, and persecuting political opponents.

The trial lasted under two hours. On the first day, Monday, January 7, the only witness for the prosecution, the police officer who interviewed the accused after their arrest, was examined by the public prosecutor and the judge. His testimony lasted about an hour. The witness submitted the only exhibit for the prosecution, the leaflet published by the Republicans on December 25, 1984. Since the accused boycotted the trial, there was nothing for the judge to do except pronounce judgment, which he postponed to the next day.

On Tuesday, the 8th of January, the judge read his judgment, which was largely based on the statements made by the accused for the investigating police officer. The judge stated that the accused held curious and unorthodox views of Islam, which might or might not be valid: according to his knowledge of Islam, the Qur'an may reveal its secrets to men of piety and diligence. Nevertheless, according to the judgment, it was certainly wrong of the accused to discuss those secrets and insights with the public, because that activity could create religious turmoil (*fitnah*).

Following this discussion of the thought of the main accused, Ustadh Mahmoud—which suggested that the judge had the Islamic offense of apostasy in mind[21]—the judgment suddenly concluded by declaring all five accused guilty of sedition, undermining the constitution, inciting unlawful opposition to the government, disturbing public tranquility, and membership in an unlawful organization. In other words, the reasoning of the decision was related to the offense of apostasy, although it never mentioned that offense by name, while the actual charges were brought on sections 96,105 and 127A of the penal code and section 20 of the State Security Act. There was no attempt in the proceedings to show how the conduct of the accused rendered them culpable under those sections.[22] While violation of section 458(3) of the penal code was mentioned as one of the charges, the judgment made no mention of that section.

The judge then passed the death sentence on all five accused under section 96 of the penal code, while adding the proviso that the accused could be reprieved if they repented and recanted their views. This clearly shows that the judge was in fact convicting the accused of apostasy, because under Islamic Shari'a law repetence and disavowal of the "heretic's" views are grounds for reprieve. There was no basis for reprieve on such grounds in relation to section 96 of the penal code under which the accused were being sentenced.

In contrast to the trial court, the special court of appeal which reviewed the judgment relied heavily on the apostasy charge, which it specified by name. The special court of appeal confirmed the lower court's finding and sentence of death for all five accused for apostasy as well as the specified sections of the penal code and State Security Act. Holding that Ustadh Mahmoud was persistent in his apostasy, the court of appeal decided to deny him the opportunity to have his death sentence reprieved through repentance and recanting his views. The Court ruled that the death sentence was to be carried out on Ustadh Mahmoud immediately. The other four accused were to be allowed one month to reconsider their position. They were told that they would be pardoned if they recanted.

21. According to historical Islamic Shari'a law, apostasy is committed by a Muslim who expressly or by implication repudiates his faith in Islam. The offense was punishable by death. Several other legal consequences followed upon a finding of apostasy. See generally Peters and Devries, "Apostasy in Islam," XVII *Die Welt des Islams* 1 (Leiden: E. J. Brill, 1976–77).

22. It is difficult to imagine how the judgment could have supported conviction for the serious offenses charged, and justified the death penalty for publishing the leaflet quoted above.

The decision of the special court of appeal was announced on Tuesday, January 15, and the President of the Republic publicly announced his confirmation on Thursday, January 17, and directed the execution of Ustadh Mahmoud on Friday, January 18. Like the trial court, President Numeiri based his address to the nation on the theory of apostasy in Islamic Shari'a law, without mentioning the offense by name, when he confirmed the conviction and sentence on all five accused. As for the other four accused, the President directed that they should have only three days to repent and recant or be executed on Sunday, January 20. Following the execution of Ustadh Mahmoud on Friday morning, the four declared their intention to recant and were accordingly pardoned and allowed to go free on Saturday the 19th.

By agreeing to dismantle their organization and refrain from further propagation of the views of Ustadh Mahmoud, all of the nearly four hundred Republican men and women detained in Omdurman on the eve of the execution were released within the week. Republicans who were detained in other towns throughout the country and formally charged with the same combination of offenses as Ustadh Mahmoud were released upon signing a similar pledge. Presumably the authorities thought that after the execution of Ustadh Mahmoud, the movement would simply cease to exist, assuming that he was its entire substance and motivating force.

President Numeiri did not stay in power long enough to reap the dubious benefits of his ruthless campaign against the Republicans. He was overthrown by a popular uprising followed by a coup d'etat on April 6, 1985, seventy-six days after he killed Ustadh Mahmoud. Far from marking the end of his thought, I believe that the events of January 1985 helped publicize and enhance the importance of Ustadh Mahmoud's work. But before turning to review his main thesis and its implications in light of his life and death, it is interesting to note the unprecedented events of that fateful Friday morning.

As President Numeiri was making his confirmation address through national radio and television on the afternoon of Thursday, January 17, 1985, all security forces in the capital were put on full alert. While the police and state security personnel were rounding up Republicans for detention without charge, the armed forces were taking charge of security in and around the central prison in Khartoum North, where the execution was to take place the following morning. Paratroops were moved inside the prison, where a helicopter was kept overnight in order to remove the body after the execution. At dawn on Friday, the largest security operation ever undertaken around the prison was mounted, as authorities checked identities and closely observed the several hundred people who came to watch the public execution scheduled for ten that morning.

When Ustadh Mahmoud was brought up the stairs of the red steel gallows, the hood covering his face was removed for a few minutes. He is reported to have surveyed the crowd with a smile before the hood was replaced for the actual execution.[23] Following the execution by hanging, the body was brought down, placed on a stretcher, and covered with an old blanket. Then it was taken to the helicopter, which immediately flew off to an unknown destination. Later it was reported that the body was buried in a shallow hole somewhere in the desert west of Omdurman. There are doubts now that even the men who carried out that bizarre operation can identify the spot where the body was left on that day.[24]

Following the overthrow of Numeiri and enactment of a new Transitional Constitution in October of 1985, a constitutional suit was instituted by Ustadh Mahmoud's elder daughter, Asma, and one of the Republicans convicted with him in the January 1985 trial. In this suit the applicants petition the Supreme Court of the Sudan to set aside the convictions and nullify their consequences based on numerous constitutional and procedural objections to that trial. The attorney general of the transitional government made an oral declaration before the Supreme Court to the effect that the January 1985 trial was completely illegal and that, as the current government's attorney, he had nothing to say in defense of that trial.[25] Nevertheless, the Supreme Court asked for a detailed written response to the petition. After considering all the available evidence and the submissions of both sides, the Supreme Court ruled that the trial, confirmation proceedings, and execution of Ustadh Mahmoud were all null and void. In a long judgment handed down on November 18, 1986, the Supreme Court discussed in detail the numerous

23. This account of the execution was reported by several foreign newspapers at the time, including American, British, and some French newspapers and magazines. See, for example the *New York Times* for January 19, 1985, p. 2.

24. It is interesting to note that *Ustadh* Mahmoud had left written instructions, during his self-imposed religious seclusion of 1948–51, that if he should die, he should be buried with the clothes he was wearing, without the usual rites of burial, and in an unmarked grave.

25. *Al-Ayyam* daily newspaper of April 18, 1986. The Sudan was ruled by a transitional government between April 1985 and April 1986. A new elected government came to power in May 1986.

faults of the whole episode, including clear violations of fundamental, constitutionally guaranteed safeguards and violations of the 1983 "Islamic" laws themselves.

In conclusion it is worth noting the overriding fear President Numeiri apparently had of this single unarmed pacifist. The circumstances of the prosecution and trial and the disproportionately severe sentence imposed for publishing a mildly worded single sheet of paper critical of government policy suggest the existence of a conspiracy or prearranged plan to murder Ustadh Mahmoud.[26] This theory draws support from the language of correspondence between President Numeiri and his top judicial and legal advisers prior to the arrest of Ustadh Mahmoud on January 5, 1985.[27]

In contrast, there is the remarkable ease and comfort with which Ustadh Mahmoud met his fate. This aspect of the episode is more significant, because it put to the ultimate test one of the main tenets of Ustadh Mahmoud's religious thinking, namely the doctrine of absolute submission to the will of God. Throughout his life he preached that submission to the will of God was the essence of Islam and endeavored to achieve such submission in every aspect of his private and public life.[28]

26. The full text of the leaflet has been quoted above. It is difficult to imagine a conspiracy between the head of a modern constitutional state and its independent judiciary to murder a person through the judicial process, but Sudan was not a modern constitutional state in January 1985, and the judiciary had totally lost its independence through gradual erosion since the late 1970s, and especially under the Judiciary Acts of 1983 and 1984. Under those two acts, the president of the republic, who was also the president of the High Judiciary Council, had the power to appoint any person to any judicial office, regardless of the qualifications required for judicial appointments under the same acts. The president in fact hand-picked and appointed a handful of judges for the capital, including Hassan Ibrahim al-Mahalawy, who "tried" Ustadh Mahmoud, and the special court of appeal, which confirmed the conviction and sentence. The numerous procedural and substantive errors which rendered that exercise a total miscarriage of justice are discussed in an article by the author of this introduction entitled: "The Islamic Law of Apostasy and its Modern Applicability: A Case from the Sudan" 16 *Religion* 197 (1986).

27. Abdel Wahab Mohamed Abdel Wahab, a well-known attorney in Khartoum with no affiliation with the Republicans, disclosed his discovery of such correspondence. Beside publishing the photocopy of one of those documents, *Al-Ayyam* daily newspaper of May 22, 1985, reported the intention of Advocate Abdel Wahab to prosecute former President Numeiri and some of his aides on charges of conspiracy to murder Ustadh Mahmoud, but the Republicans objected to such a prosecution, and the idea was overtaken by other events. Although this prosecution never materialized, the issue has been raised in the constitutional suit referred to above.

28. Here I speak from personal experience as a close associate of the man for seventeen years. The word *Islam* in Arabic means submission, and the theme of submission is recurrent in the Qur'an and Muslim traditions as the proof of genuine piety.

He often told his disciples to see the hand of the original actor, God, behind that of the apparent actor or immediate cause of the event or incident. By accepting his fate in that manner, Ustadh Mahmoud demonstrated that belief and action can combine in the life of a human being into a single consistent pattern, even up to the ultimate test of death. To many Sudanese, and perhaps eventually to the world at large, when his life and work are fully appreciated, the events of that fateful Friday morning are the most eloquent testimony to the extraordinary moral stature of the man.

THE MAIN IMPLICATIONS OF THE SECOND MESSAGE

For the benefit of readers who may not be familiar with Islamic history, the main relevant features of that history may be briefly stated here in order to put Ustadh Mahmoud's work in context. The Prophet Mohamed was born in Mecca, a town in western Arabia, around 570 A.D. At the age of forty he began receiving revelation, the Qur'an, which is believed by Muslims to be the literal and final word of God. For thirteen years the Prophet preached the faith to his own tribe, Qurysh, and other Arabs who used to frequent Mecca as a leading religious and commercial center at the time. Then, in the face of the growing hostility of Qurysh, culminating in a plot to kill the Prophet himself, in 622 Mohamed and his few followers migrated to Medina, another town in western Arabia. The Qur'an continued to be revealed for a total of twenty-three years, thirteen years in Mecca and ten years in Medina, up to the Prophet's death in 632 A.D. Throughout this period, the Prophet continued to explain and apply the Qur'an in response to the concrete needs of the growing Muslim community. The record of what the Prophet is believed to have said and done during that period was subsequently called Sunnah, the second source of Islam.[29]

The first Islamic state was established in Medina through an alliance between the migrants and their supporters in Medina, together with the Christian and Jewish tribes of the area. During that initial period, Christians and Jews, known as Ahl al-Kitab, People of the Book, were treated with tolerance and respect as equal partners in the charter which

---

29. As will be explained in the text of this book, Ustadh Mahmoud makes a distinction between two levels of Sunnah, one level pertaining to Shari'a as promulgated for use by the community at large, while the other level pertains to the Prophet's own superior standards of conduct.

regulated their relationship with the Muslims.[30] Provided they submitted to the Prophet as ruler of the community, they were to enjoy protection of their persons and property and allowed to practice their religions. When the Jews violated that charter, according to Muslim historical records, the Prophet punished them and severely restricted their rights.[31] The growing popularity of Islam and the consequent strength of the Muslim state enabled the Prophet to march back into Mecca unopposed and consolidate his rule over most of Arabia before his death in 632 A.D.

Following the Prophet's death, his leading companion, Abu Bakr, was chosen, with some difficulty, as his successor. Differences as to who was entitled to succeed the Prophet as ruler of the Islamic state led to strife and civil war within a couple of decades, and they continue to divide Muslims to the present day. The Shi'a sect of modern-day Iran and other parts of the Muslim world derive their origins from the party which supported Ali, the Prophet's cousin and son-in-law, as leader of the Muslims.

Although the Qur'an itself was recorded during the reign of Osman, the third *Khalifa* or successor of the Prophet, the second source of Islam, the Sunnah, was not recorded until the second and third centuries of Islam. For the first few generations, Muslims accepted the moral and religious authority of the Prophet's companions, *sahabah*, and their successors, *tab'in*, with their assumed knowledge of the oral traditions of the Prophet. With the recording of Sunnah and the development of *usul al-fiqh*, the science of Islamic jurisprudence for deriving general principles and specific rules from the fundamental sources, the scene was set for the articulation and tabulation of the general principles and detailed rules of Shari'a. The leading surviving schools of orthodox Islamic jurisprudence were founded in the second and third centuries of Islam. Al-Tabari, who is generally recognized as the last founder of an independent school of Islamic jurisprudence, died in 923 A.D.

In this way, the law which came to be known as Shari'a was created through the interpretation by jurists of the fundamental sources of Islam, mainly the Qur'an and Sunnah, during the eighth and ninth centuries

30. For a translation of this charter see M. Watt, *Islamic Political Thought* (Edinburgh: Edinburgh University Press, 1968), pp. 130–34.

31. This episode is discussed in, for example, B. Lewis, *The Arabs in History* (New York: Harper and Row 1960), p. 40ff., and F. Gabrielli, *Muhammad and the Conquest of Islam* trans. by V. Luling and R. Linell (New York: World University Library, McGraw-Hill Co., 1968), pp. 64–80.

A.D. From the tenth century up to the present time, Muslim jurists have confined themselves to the study and elaboration of the work of those early masters. Even the intermediate reformers, such as Ibn Taymiya, who died in 1328 A.D., and the modern reformers of the last and present centuries, such as Mohamed Abdu and Jamal al-Din al-Afghany, have accepted the main principles set by the established orthodox schools of Islamic jurisprudence and complied with the acceptable processes of reform as determined by the early jurists.

Without going into the theological arguments which are the subject of this book, the main thesis of Ustadh Mahmoud regarding the evolution of Islamic law may be summarized as follows. Islam, being the final and universal religion according to Muslim belief, was offered first in tolerant and egalitarian terms in Mecca, where the Prophet preached equality and individual responsibility between all men and women without distinction on grounds of race, sex, or social origin. As that message was rejected in practice, and the Prophet and his few followers were persecuted and forced to migrate to Medina, some aspects of the message changed in response to the socioeconomic and political realities of the time. Migration to Medina (hijrah) was not merely a tactical step, but also signified a shift in the content of the message itself. The difference is clearly shown in close examination and comparison of the Qur'anic texts and Sunnah dating from the Mecca stage and those following the migration to Medina. Texts from both periods are contained in the fundamental sources of Islam, namely the Qur'an and Sunnah; the difference is in the level of the audience being addressed and the society and particular class of texts was supposed to regulate.

Historical Islamic Shari'a law as known to the Muslims today was based on texts of the second stage. In the Medina stage God was responding, through the Prophet in the Qur'an and Sunnah, to the potential and actual needs of human society at that stage of its development. To that end, some aspects of the earlier level of revelation and Sunnah were subjected to repeal or abrogation (naskh) from the legal point of view, although they remained operative at a moral/persuasive level. This much is readily accepted by most Muslims, although some may object to the candid language in which these developments were discussed by Ustadh Mahmoud. What is revolutionary in his thinking, however, is the notion that the abrogation process (naskh) was in fact a postponement and not final and conclusive repeal. Once this basic premise is conceded, a whole new era of Islamic jurisprudence can begin, one that allows for the development of complete liberty and equality for all human beings, regardless of sex, religion, or faith. As it stands now, historical Islamic Shari'a law does in fact discriminate on grounds of sex and religion.

Under historical Shari'a rules of personal status, for example, a man has the right to marry up to four wives and the right to divorce any of them at will. There is no need for him to comply with any procedural or substantive requirements, or even to reveal his reasons. In contrast, a woman can only obtain a divorce by judicial decree within very strict and limited causes for divorce. Furthermore, women under Shari'a law suffer a variety of civil limitations, such as disqualification from holding certain types of public office and from testifying in certain types of judicial proceedings, even when their own rights are at issue.

Religious discrimination under historical Shari'a law derives from the fact that Shari'a classifies people in terms of their religious beliefs and apportions civil and political rights accordingly.[32] Muslims, at one end of the scale, enjoy the full range of rights accorded to a citizen by Shari'a. An unbeliever, at the other end, has no rights whatsoever, except under temporary license or safe-conduct (aman). Non-Muslim believers, mainly Christians and Jews, may be offered a compact of dhimma, whereby they enjoy security of person and property, and a degree of communal autonomy in matters of personal status, in exchange for payment of a special personal tax (jiziah). A person who is "tolerated" within a Muslim state under a compact of dhimma also suffers a variety of civil disqualifications in relation to competence to hold public office or testify in judicial proceedings.

The fact that Shari'a does not treat women and non-Muslims equally with male Muslims is beyond dispute. Beside seeking to justify such discrimination in apologetic terms,[33] modern Muslim scholars claim that some of the objectionable rules may now be reformed by reviving the techniques of creative juristic reasoning (ijtihad). None of these scholars, however, claims that such reform can possibly remove all discrimination

32. See generally, Majid Khadduri, War and Peace in the Law of Islam (Johns Hopkins University Press, 1955), chapters 14 and 17 and H. A. R. Gibb and J. H. Kramers, eds., Shorter Encyclopaedia of Islam (Leiden: E. J. Brill, 1953), pp. (16–17, 75–76, 91–92, 205–206 and 542–544 .

33. The term "Muslim apologetics" was coined by Professor W. C. Smith. (See his book, Islam in Modern History [Princeton University Press, 1967].) For critical review of these reform efforts see also H. A. R. Gibb, Modern Trends in Islam (Chicago University Press, 1947) and Malcolm Kerr, Islamic Reform (University of California Press, 1966).

against women and non-Muslims, because *ijtihad* itself has its limitations. In particular, *ijtihad* is not permitted in any matter governed by an explicit and definite text of the Qur'an or Sunnah.[34] It therefore follows that any discriminatory rule that is based on an explicit and definite text—and some of the most obviously discriminatory rules are in fact based on such texts as Qur'an or Sunnah—is not open to reform through *ijtihad* or any other technique known to historical Shari'a.

This presents the modern Muslim with a real and serious dilemma: either implement historical Shari'a with its discrimination against women and non-Muslims, or discard Shari'a in public life and seek to establish a secular state. Both options are untenable in the modern Muslim world. The realities of domestic and international relations make implementation of the first option impracticable, while the religious obligation of Muslims to conduct every aspect of their public as well as private life in accordance with Islamic teachings would not permit the second.[35] The only way out of this dilemma, argued Ustadh Mahmoud, is to evolve Islamic law to a fresh plane rather than waste time in piecemeal reform that will never achieve the moral and political objective of removing all discrimination against women and non-Muslims in Islamic law.

Starting with the premise explained and substantiated in this book, *The Second Message of Islam*, namely, that historical Shari'a is not the whole of Islam but merely the level of Islamic law that suited the previous stage of human development, Ustadh Mahmoud proposed to shift certain aspects of Islamic law from their foundation in one class of texts of the Qur'an and Sunnah and place them on a different class of texts of the Qur'an and Sunnah. The limitations of reform noted above are removed by reviving the earlier texts, which were never made legally binding in the past, and making them the basis of modern Islamic law. Explicit and definite texts of the Qur'an and Sunnah that were the basis of discrimination against women and non-Muslims under historical Shari'a are set aside as having served their transitional purpose. Other texts of the Qur'an and Sunnah are made legally binding in order to achieve full equality for all human beings, regardless of sex or religion. This shift is

34. The Sunnah which provides authority for the exercise of *ijtihad*, the Prophet's instruction to Ma'adh ibn Jabal when he appointed him governor of Yemen, describes *ijtihad* as a last resort, to be exercised only when no explicit and definite ruling can be found in the Qur'an or Sunnah.

35. On this religious obligation, see, for example, Qur'an chapter 4 verse 59 and chapter 33 verse 36.

made possible through examining the rationale of abrogation (*naskh*) in the sense of selecting which texts of the Qur'an and Sunnah are to be made legally binding, as opposed to being merely morally persuasive.

In *The Second Message of Islam*, Ustadh Mahmoud explained his main thesis for the evolution of modern Islamic law. In other writings and throughout his life, he articulated and developed this fundamental principle, which provides the ideological basis for his position on a wide range of social or political issues. The principle of the evolution of Islamic Shari'a law, as the Arabic term may be translated, was not Ustadh Mahmoud's only contribution. More fundamental to his work, in my view, is his essentially religious view of the universe and the role of humans in the cosmic order of things. That aspect of his work is covered in general terms in the first three chapters of this book and receives more extensive treatment in his specialized books, such as *Risalat al-Salah* (A Treatise on Prayer) and *Al-Qur'an wa Mustafa Mahmoud wa al-Fahm al-'Asry* (The Modern Understanding of the Qur'an), written in response to the writings of the Egyptian author Mustafa Mahmoud.[36] It is in the context of such writings that the splendid combination of spirituality and rationality of his thought may best be appreciated. The unity and consistency that characterize his approach to every moral and secular, public and private, domestic and global issue and his ability to practice what he preached shall long remain, in my view, high examples of human excellence.

Another major theme in his work is the relationship between the achievement of inner peace within the individual person as an essential prerequisite to the achievement of peace with all other beings in society and the world at large. Since he perceived religion to be the most effective means of achieving such peace within the individual person, he maintained that resort to religion has become a matter of life and death for the whole human race, faced with the prospect of total extinction (or at least the end of all civilization as we know it today) in the event of global nuclear war.

Given the urgent and intriguing nature of these and other issues discussed in *The Second Message of Islam*, it is clear that this book will interest readers of all cultural and religious traditions, including agnostics

36. The first book was first published in January 1966, with an extensive introduction added in the fourth edition. The second book was first published in January 1971. Both books are available only in Arabic at the present time.

and atheists, who should not prematurely dismiss it out of hand as yet another religious argument. In view of the failure of secular philosophy to satisfy our basic material and spiritual needs, religion deserves a closer look, especially when it is offered in such a refreshingly open-minded and enlightened manner.

IMMEDIATE IMPACT AND FUTURE PROSPECTS

At the immediate local level, the legacy of Ustadh Mahmoud is best reflected in the moral and intellectual transformation of female Republicans. He often said that his work was his female disciples. Young educated Muslim women found in the ideas of Ustadh Mahmoud an Islamic answer to their social and spiritual needs, and they participated effectively in the work of the movement. Many educated Muslim males have also found these ideas appealing and committed themselves to their propagation throughout the Sudan.

As can be expected, the same features which made the work of Ustadh Mahmoud appealing to these groups and to non-Muslim Sudanese are the basis of the fierce hostility of the orthodox Islamic establishment. Republican publications recorded and analyzed numerous heated debates with the orthodox Islamic scholars of the official Sudanese Department of Religious Affairs, traditional sectarian leaders, and the fundamentalist Muslim Brotherhood who advocate the total imposition of historical Shari'a. The animosity and pressure exerted by these groups were no doubt one of the main causes of ex-President Numeiri's decision to execute Ustadh Mahmoud. As the result of the elections of April 1986, these groups are now in power in the Sudan. They have not yet moved against the Republicans, possibly because the latter have kept a low political profile since the execution of their leader. Should the Republicans continue to pose a political threat to the traditionalists and fundamentalists in power, one can expect harsh consequences to follow.

The inaction of Republicans since the death of Ustadh Mahmoud may be understood in light of the tremendous shock of the loss of the founder and leader of their movement. If this initial organizational and leadership crisis continues for long, however, one may wonder about the group's ability to continue the work of their revered teacher. If they should fail, that would not necessarily, of course, mean the end of his influence. Many great religious and ideological missions in the past have found wide acceptance and concrete application many years after the death of their founders, and often in foreign lands.

Besides this long-term broader impact, to which we shall return below, the life and death of Ustadh Mahmoud have already had direct and substantial political consequences. In this regard one may note, for example, the effect of Ustadh Mahmoud's execution in initiating the sequence of events that brought the overthrow of Numeiri and the significance of the commemoration of his execution a year later.

On the eve of the confirmation of Ustadh Mahmoud's death sentence, a committee of professional and labor union leaders met in the University of Khartoum to organize efforts to protest the trial and seek a stay of execution. When that effort failed, the same committee continued to organize the mass demonstrations and general strike which brought Numeiri's rule to an end seventy-six days later. The grotesque spectacle of the political trial and execution of this respected pacifist Islamic intellectual was taken by hundreds of thousands of Sudanese as final proof of the depths to which Numeiri himself had sunk.[37] In this way, the execution of Ustadh Mahmoud can be seen as the trigger which activated the democratic movement directly leading to Numeiri's downfall.

To reaffirm their view of the man as a symbol for a renewed commitment to democratic freedoms, thousands of intellectuals and professionals participated in the week of public lectures and debates held in January 1986 to commemorate what they described as the martyrdom of Ustadh Mahmoud. On the same occasion, the 18th of January was declared by the Arab Human Rights organization, headquartered in Cairo, to be the Arab Human Rights Day in honor of Ustadh Mahmoud.[38] Such recognition of his achievements by non-Republicans clearly reflects the great and enduring value of his work. This is not surprising, because that work responds to genuine individual and collective needs for freedom and justice on the national as well as the international levels.

The broader, long-term significance of Ustadh Mahmoud's work for the many Muslim countries facing the prospects of the total application of Shari'a can hardly be exaggerated. In the context of the Sudan, for example, not only women but also the non-Muslim Sudanese, approximately one-third of the population, stand to lose many of the fundamen-

37. Ann M. Lesch, *The Fall of Numeiri,* Universities Field Staff International Reports (1985) No. 9, Africa, at p. 11.

38. *Al-Sahafa* and *Al-Ayyam 1* daily newspapers of December 22, 1985. All major Sudanese newspapers reported in detail the activities of the week, January 11 to January 18, 1986, and published numerous articles and features to mark the occasion.

tal rights which they used to take for granted under the secular legal system prevailing up to 1983. The imposition of Shari'a was one of the primary causes of the resumption of the civil war in 1983, after ten years of peace and stability in the southern part of the country.[39] If Shari'a is to be applied in strict compliance with its historical formulation, even male Muslims will suffer a degrading of their civil and political rights. Shari'a's constitutional theory provides for extensive, practically unlimited powers of the ruler, who combines ultimate executive, judicial, and legislative powers, insofar as these can be held in human hands. He is theoretically bound by Shari'a, but because he holds the final say over its interpretation and application, including the power to make regulations to supplement Shari'a, the ruler of an Islamic state based on the Shari'a model is, in effect, an absolute ruler. Moreover, there is no provision in Shari'a for legal political opposition and orderly transfer of power.

Given these and other very serious implications for constitutional government and the rule of law in the modern sense of these terms, it is not surprising to find that *The Second Message of Islam* is particularly appealing to women, non-Muslims, and liberal educated Muslims in general. Despite the growing popularity of the Republican ideology in the Sudan over the last decade, however, the core membership of the group still remains relatively small. Thousands of close sympathizers among the educated Muslim elites seem to be intimidated by the forces of established religious and political orthodoxy. As they begin to appreciate the full implications of an Islamic state on the traditionalist and fundamentalist Shari'a model, however, they are most likely to opt, I would suggest, for Ustadh Mahmoud's alternative Islamic interpretation. Non-Muslim Sudanese, on the other hand, have their own religious and cultural reservations to any Islamic approach. Their first preference would therefore be a secular state. Once they are faced with a choice between competing Islamic ideologies, as seems to be the case in Sudan now, they too would opt, I suggest, for that of Ustadh Mahmoud, because it provides an Islamic basis for the constitutional benefits of secularism, despite its

39. On the eve of independence on the first of January 1956, civil war broke out in the southern Sudan, and continued, intermittently, until it was settled through the Addis Ababa Agreement of 1972. On the violation of that Agreement by Numeiri in 1982–83, by attempting to redivide the southern region and imposing Shari'a, the civil war was resumed in the South. On what is known as the southern problem see, for example, Mohamed Omer Beshir, *The Southern Sudan: Background to Conflict* (London: C. Hurst and Co., 1968) and *The Southern Sudan: From Conflict to Peace* (New York: Barnes and Noble, 1975).

strongly religious orientation. Similar choices, I would submit, will probably be made by women, non-Muslims, and liberally minded Muslims elsewhere. The writings of Ustadh Mahmoud are already being read and appreciated in other parts of the Arab Muslim world. With the publication of this and other translations of his books, his ideas will now reach a global audience.

In other words, conditions are ripe for a keen and fruitful interest in the work of Ustadh Mahmoud. Despite the unfortunate cost in human terms, the Muslim experience with the so-called fundamentalist regimes and policies in Iran, Pakistan, and the Sudan over the last few years have perhaps done as much to promote the cause of the Second Message of Islam as have the Republicans over the last forty years. The futility and brutality of these regimes and policies have provided valuable practical illustration of the untenability of historical Shari'a under modern conditions. In this way, Muslims are forced to reexamine ancient concepts and assumptions in the light of the concrete realities of life today.

Resort to secular ideology, as indicated above, is unlikely, because of the Muslims' religious obligation to regulate all aspects of their public and private life in accordance with the principles of Islam. To seek secular answers is simply to abandon the field to the fundamentalists, who will succeed in carrying the vast majority of the population with them by citing religious authority for their policies and theories. Intelligent and enlightened Muslims are therefore best advised to remain within the religious framework and endeavor to achieve the reforms that would make Islam a viable modern ideology.

TRANSLATOR'S NOTE

With all the assistance and encouragement I have received from many able friends and colleagues, I still had much difficulty preparing this translation and am not sure I have succeeded in fully achieving all that I set out to do. It may be helpful to note here some of the problems I faced and the answers I decided to adopt.

The Second Message of Islam is based on a modern and revolutionary interpretation of the Qur'an. It is generally agreed that the Qur'an itself is impossible to translate because of the multiplicity and subtlety of shades of meanings in the original Arabic text. Moreover, the musical and emotional impact of the Qur'an cannot be rendered by even the most skillful and poetic translation. The task of translating a work interpreting the untranslatable text of the Qur'an is further complicated by the fact that this book often deals with the deeper metaphorical and metaphysical meanings of the Qur'an (ta'wyl).

Another source of difficulty relates to my own limitations. Beside lacking professional training or experience in translation as such, I am further constrained from undertaking significant interpretation of or deviation from the Arabic text for fear of distorting or misrepresenting the views of the author who has been and continues to be my spiritual mentor. I have therefore attempted the closest and most literal translation, with as little deviation from the Arabic text as possible. This is not necessarily a fault, but should nevertheless be noted in case the reader sometimes wonders about the lack of fluency in style. For this I can only apologize and hope that my translation will stimulate enough interest for a more able person to undertake a better translation of this or some other book by Ustadh Mahmoud.

Finally, and before leaving the reader with the text itself, I wish to make the following remarks concerning the style and methodology adopted here.

This is a translation of the fifth edition of the book, and includes the introductions to the fourth and third editions. Although some readers may feel that there is some repetition, both introductions are extremely useful in explaining key issues discussed in the text.

As indicated above, I deliberately tried to be as literal as possible, to avoid introducing any personal interpretation or distortion of the subject matter.

Again, as indicated above, Qur'anic texts are difficult to translate, especially when referred to in their deeper and more metaphorical sense. I have sought help from several published interpretations of the Qur'an, but found none of them completely adequate for my purpose. In the end, I decided to use my own version, in order to bring out what I know, from other sources and long association, to be the author's purpose in quoting the text.

In an attempt to address the widest possible readership, I have kept the number of Arabic terms to a minimum. Frequently used Arabic words and phrases are included in a glossary for easy reference.

There is unfortunately no agreement on a single set of rules of transliteration from Arabic into English. In general, I have attempted to follow as much as possible the American National Standard for the Romanization of Arabic,[40] except for some commonly known words and proper names.

40. American National Standards Institute, Inc., New York, N.Y., 1972.

Because of all the cooperation and assistance I received in preparing this translation, it could well be described as a collaborative work. I do accept responsibility for any failings, however, since I exercised my own judgment in drafting the original version and rejecting some comments and suggestions. I wish to acknowledge in particular the efforts of Abdel Mutalib B. Zahran, Khalid al-Haj, Mu'tasim Mahmoud, Abdullah Ernest Johnson, Khalid Duran, Al-Tayb Hassan, and Abdel Mun'im Al-Rawy. I am also grateful to Dr. Richard P. Stevens and Mrs. Jane Hager, who read drafts of this translation and made numerous corrections and improvements.

A substantial part of the work on this translation was done during my stay at the Center for the Study of Human Rights, Columbia University, New York City, as a Rockefeller Fellow in Human Rights in 1981–82. I sincerely appreciate the help and support rendered to me by the Center. I am also grateful for a grant from the Ford Foundation, which enabled me to do some revisions of the first draft. The final draft was prepared during my appointment as Visiting Professor of Law at the University of California, Los Angeles, in 1985–86. I am grateful for the help and support of the School. In particular, I am grateful to Ms. Margaret Kiever, who typed the whole manuscript and undertook the tedious process of revision and correction most ably and graciously.

Introduction to the Fourth Edition

In the name of God, the Beneficent, the Merciful

There is no compulsion in religion; guidance and error have been clearly distinguished; he who rejects false deities, and believes in God, has a hold on a secure handle which shall never break, and God is All-Hearing and All-Knowing. (2:256)[1]

And he who submits himself to God, intelligently and knowingly, has grasped the secure handle, and to God everything shall return. (31:22)

This is the introduction to the fourth edition of *The Second Message of Islam*. The first edition, published in January 1967, in the revered month of Ramadan 1386 (A.H.), has attained considerable popularity. Since that time interest in this work has increased remarkably, as its relevance to modern life has become increasingly apparent.

This book is the basic text for the "Republican Cause." Yet it is extremely concise. Further explanation and elaboration will follow in good time, God willing.

It is not my purpose in this introduction to discuss in detail any of the book's different themes. I wish, however, at the outset, to emphasize and clarify an important point, namely, that Islam consists of two messages: a First message based on the subsidiary texts of the Qur'an, and a Second Message based on the primary texts of the Qur'an. The First Message has already been interpreted and elaborated, while the Second Message still awaits interpretation and elaboration. That shall be done when its man

---

1. Qur'anic texts are cited by quoting the number of the chapter followed by the number of the verse. Thus, this first citation comes from verse number 256 of Chapter 2.

and its people come:2 "That is an absolute imperative of your Lord." (19:71)

THE SECURE HANDLE

Al-'rwah is the hold, or the handle from which an object may be carried. It is also the knot at the end of the rope through which the holder fastens his grip on the rope. Al-'rwat al-wthqa is thus the secure handle of a secure rope. The rope is religion. God said:

> Resort to the rope of God all of you, and do not disperse, and remember the grace of God conferred upon you, as you were enemies and he reconciled your hearts, thereby you became through His grace as brothers, and you were on the brink of a pit of hell, and He saved you from it. That is how He explains His signs to you, so that you may be guided. (3:103)

The rope here is Islam, and it is the Qur'an, which means the same thing. Ali ibn Abu-Talib reported the following dialogue with the Prophet:

> [The Prophet said that] there shall be upheaval. I asked: What will be the way out, O Messenger of God? He replied: the Book of God! It contains the tales of those who preceded you, and the news of what shall follow, and the rule on what prevails amongst you. . . . It is the ultimate, and it should never be taken lightly. . . . Anyone who abandons it out of arrogance, God shall humiliate him, and anyone who seeks guidance elsewhere, God shall misguide him. It is the secure rope of God, the wise message and straight path. It is guaranteed against false direction or misinterpretation. The knowledgeable shall never have enough of it, and it shall never wear by continuous use, nor shall its wonders cease. When the demons listened to it, they said: We have heard a wonderful Qur'an that guides to the straight path. Anyone who quotes it tells the truth, anyone who applies it shall do justice, and anyone who is invited to it is being invited to the straight path.

---

2. That is to say, the man who has the religious authority to interpret and elaborate, and the people who have the capacity and ability to implement, the Second Message of Islam.

This rope has descended from God in His infinitude to people on earth. Its beginning is with us, but its end is with God, in His infinitude. This image is explained in the best possible way by God at the beginning of chapter 43: "Ha-Mim. I swear by the clarifying Book, We have rendered it into Arabic so that you may understand. It is with Us in its origin as supreme and wise." (43:2–3) This rope is also called the guidance in the verse where God addresses *Iblis* (Satan), Eve, and Adam: "We said: 'Go forth hence, all of you. And if there comes to you guidance from me, then whoso shall follow My guidance, on them [shall come] no fear nor shall they grieve.'"(2:38) This guidance descended from God in His infinitude to the bottom, to which *Iblis*, Eve, and Adam had fallen, namely, the earth. This is what makes guidance, and the rope, one and the same thing, which is the Qur'an.

"Al-'rwat al-wthqa," which we said is the secure handle of the strong rope, is really the end of the rope that touches the earth—the earth of people. This is the message according to the ostensible (*zahir*) meaning of the Qur'an revealed by the Arabic language, expressed by God in the phrase: "We have rendered it into Arabic so that you may understand." The expression "so that you may understand" connotes its descent to the level of reality on earth, that is, of Shari'a. This strong rope descended from infinitude. God described its point of descent by saying: "It is with Us in its origin as supreme and wise." He also refers to its point of descent at infinitude by saying "Ha-Mim," which is an extremely subtle reference,[3] while the former phrase presents an extremely eloquent expression. The difference between the two, the reference and the expression, is merely one of degree. Both refer to the same thing, namely, the Divine Being (*al-dhat*), and the differences are intended to clarify the concept.

The secure handle is Shari'a, while the strong rope is religion. The difference between Shari'a and religion is one of degree and not of kind. Shari'a is that degree of religion addressed to ordinary people in accordance with their level of understanding.

We have quoted at the beginning of this introduction two verses. The first states:

---

3. According to the author, the use of letters of the Arabic alphabet indicates the inability of language to contain all the meaning of the Qur'an, the speech of God (see Chapter 5).

There is no compulsion in religion; guidance and error have been clearly distinguished; he who rejects false deities, and believes in God, has a hold on a secure handle which shall never break, and God is All-Hearing and All-Knowing.

The secure handle is Shari'a, and it shall never break from religion for those who reject the false deities and believe in God. It is the secure path to the ultimate goal. The condition for its secure attachment to religion, however, is rejection of false deities and belief in God. This means that its fastening to religion will be broken for those who do not reject false deities or who are without belief in God, which is the situation of Muslims today. The second verse says:

And he who submits himself to God, intelligently and knowingly, has grasped the secure handle, and to God everything shall return.

This verse is similar in meaning to the first, but further emphasizes the effectiveness of Shari'a in leading one to the goal. The phrase, "And he who submits himself to God, intelligently and knowingly" corresponds to the phrase, "he who rejects false deities and believes in God" in the first verse. Then comes the phrase, "and to God everything shall return." This refers to return by ascending the rope which descends from infinitude, where man used to be before he was expelled and banished because of his error: "We said all of you shall descend from it. And when you receive guidance from Me, those who follow My guidance shall have no fear nor shall they grieve." (2:38) In the same manner God says: "We have created man in the best mold. Then We reduced him to the bottom of creation. But those who believed and did good deeds shall have unlimited reward." (95:4–6) The unlimited reward is continuous, thus it is the "secure handle which shall never break."

THE SUNNAH[4] IS THE SECOND MESSAGE

Sunnah contains Shari'a and thus exceeds it. So if the secure handle is Shari'a, Sunnah is even more secure. As the rope of Islam descends

4. The author reserves the term *Sunnah* as applicable only to the personal example of the Prophet, and not all his traditions, as is sometimes wrongly assumed. The Prophet sometimes had to approve for others standards lower than his own in view of their weakness.

from infinitude to people on earth, laying Shari'a, and addressing people according to their understanding, Sunnah is above the level of people in general. . . . It is Shari'a for the Prophet personally, addressed to him specifically, according to his level of understanding as distinguished from that of people in general. This is the difference between Sunnah and Shari'a.

The Second Message consists simply of reviving Sunnah and making it Shari'a for people in general. Through the grace of God, human society has, over the last fourteen centuries, developed a level of understanding capable of responding to this Second Message. When the Prophet prophesied the revival of Islam, he prophesied it in the sense of a revival of Sunnah, rather than that of Shari'a. He said:

"Islam started as a stranger, and it shall return as a stranger in the same way it started. . . . Blessed are the strangers! They asked: Who are the strangers, Oh Messenger of God? He replied: Those who revive my Sunnah after it had been abandoned."

It is obvious that he did not mean the revival of Shari'a, but the revival of Sunnah. Sunnah, as indicated above, contains the Shari'a, and exceeds it. . . . Sunnah is a methodology (tariqah); that is, it is a higher level of Shari'a.

SUNNAH IS NOT UNIQUE TO THE PROPHET

Islamic theologians are often quoted to the effect that a certain practice is unique to the Prophet. This is a gross misunderstanding and has negative consequences in discouraging people from following the Prophet's example. For God says on behalf of the Prophet: "Say: if you love God, then follow me, and God shall love you." (3:31) In this way, Shari'a opens up into Sunnah, and it becomes required of a diligent and purposeful worshiper to promote himself from Shari'a to *al-tariqa*, that is, Sunnah. This advancement was not, however, previously required of people in general; it was merely advised. It could not have been made obligatory in view of the dictates of the time and prevailing circumstances.

The first stage of propagation of the Message was addressed to the nation of believers (Mu'minin), while the personal life-style of the Prophet himself was one of genuine submission to God (that of Muslimin), submission being a more advanced stage than belief. In that nation of Mu'minin, the Prophet was the only true Muslim. This has been explained in the text of this book, and may be referred to therein.[5] What we need to affirm here is that modern society is preparing to receive the nation of Muslimin, which is the nation of the Second Message; its law is Sunnah of the Prophet and not Shari'a which is the law of the previous nation. As indicated above, this is due to the grace of God and the development of human society over a long time [since Islam began fourteen hundred years ago], which has rendered human society today capable of understanding the law that evolved, or developed, from the first Shari'a level to the Sunnah level. It is as if reality has been elevated during this period of time, and part of the rope has been drawn from the distance to a closer point, thereby placing the new secure handle closer to infinitude than the old one. This is due to the proximity of the understanding of ordinary people today to infinitude in comparison to the previous level of understanding.

The nation of Muslimin is what the Prophet called the Brothers, while he called the Companions the nation of Mu'minin. In his well-known *Hadith*, he said:

> How I long for my Brothers who have not come yet. They said: Are we not your Brothers, O Messenger of God? He replied: No, you are my Companions. . . . How I long for my brothers who have not come yet. They said: Are we not your brothers, O Messenger of God? He replied: No, you are my companions. How I long for my brothers who have not come yet! They asked: Who are your brothers? He replied: A people who come at the end of time, of whom the active one shall have seventy times as much reward as you have. They asked: Seventy times as much as we have or they have? He replied: As you have. They asked: Why? He replied: Because you find assistance in doing good, and they find no assistance.

The Prophet also said of the Brothers in another context "The prophets are sons of the same mother," meaning that they are brothers because they all suckle from the same breast, namely, the breast *"la ilah ila-Allah."*[6] This means that the members of the nation of Muslimin shall be as knowledgeable of God as if they were prophets, although they are not prophets [since they receive no fresh revelation].

5. The crucial distinction between *Mu'minin* (believers) and *Muslimin* (genuine submitters or surrenders to God) is explained on pages 46–47 in detail.

6. This phrase literally means there is no god but God, or that God is the only Lord and Creator, that is, that He is the sole actor and creator of all things and actions, big and small.

The claim that Sunnah is peculiar to the Prophet is repudiated by the verse: "You have received a messenger from amongst yourselves who is deeply distressed by your suffering, cares for you, and he is tender and merciful to the believers." (9:128) The key to this verse, the phrase "from amongst yourselves," indicates that the perfections of the Prophet are for all to achieve if his method is followed, because he is of our kind and not of an alien kind. The difference between him and any of us is one of degree and not of kind. To say that a practice or activity is peculiar to the Prophet misses the wisdom of having prophets sent from amongst human beings rather than angels.

The world today, with all its tremendous material capabilities and excellent human and material advancement, together with all this confusion of the hearts and minds of people, is no doubt preparing for the emergence of the nation of Muslimin. It is therefore the duty of the inheritors of Islam, the inheritors of the Qur'an, to proclaim the Second Message in anticipation of the new era for which humanity feels a desperate need and to which it is unable to find the way. The way is the Qur'an, which of course does not speak: men must speak for it. God says in this connection: "It [the Qur'an] is clear signs in the hearts of those who are given knowledge, and none but the unfair ones deny Our signs." (29:49)

The phrase "the hearts of those who are given the knowledge" points the way to the new era, the way of the Muslimin on earth, as laid down in the primary texts of the Qur'an, those revealed in Mecca, which were repealed or abrogated during the first stage of Islam by the subsidiary texts—those revealed in Medina.[7] The primary texts were abrogated then because of the dictates of the time (hukm al-waqt), as it was the time for the nation of Mu'minin. The primary texts address the nation of Muslimin, which did not come into being at that time.

The primary texts were repealed or abrogated, in the sense of being postponed, and suspended in relation to legislation until their proper time, which has dawned upon us now. That is why we have applied ourselves to the proclamation of the Second Message.

THE SECOND MESSAGE OF ISLAM

Islam is one religion, the Religion of God, for which He accepts no alternative. God says in this respect: "Do they seek other than the Religion of God, to Whom all those in heavens and earth have already

7. The rationale and significance of the process of abrogation is explained in chapters 5 and 6.

surrendered, whether willingly or unwillingly, and to Whom they shall return?" (3:83)

Islam, in this sense, is total and contented submission to God as the Lord. All the prophets since Adam and up to Mohamed came with Islam. God says in this respect:

> He has ordained for you the Religion which He enjoined to Noah, and which We revealed to you, and what We enjoined to Abraham and Moses and Jesus: Establish Religion and do not disperse in it. It is very difficult for the infidels [to accept] what you invite them to [accept], God chooses for Himself whom He wishes, and guides to Himself he who turns [to Him]. (42:13)

The phrase "He has ordained for you the Religion" in this context does not mean Shari'a laws, but rather that God is the only true God and creator (la ilah ila-Allah), because the laws of all nations are not the same, as they differ in degree due to the differences between the nations, while la ilah ila-Allah is permanent, though in form only and not in substance, as such substance varies with the levels of the Messenger, which is another difference of degree. The Prophet expressed the permanence of la ilah ila-Allah in the following terms: "The best that I and other prophets before me brought is la ilah ila-Allah."

The difference in the Shari'a laws of the prophets, because of differences in the levels of understanding of their nations, should be clear enough. Suffice to remind the reader of the difference in matrimonial laws between Adam and Mohamed. While in Adam's time Islamic Shari'a allowed marriage of a brother to his own sister, the permissible became prohibited in the Shari'a of Mohamed. Moreover, the prohibition extended even further. God stated the rule:

> Forbidden to you are your mothers, and your daughters, and your sisters, and your fathers' sisters, and your mothers' sisters, and brother's daughters, and sister's daughters and your foster-mothers that have given you suck, and your foster-sisters, and the mothers of your wives, and your step-daughters, who are your wards being born of your wives to whom you have gone in—but if you have not gone in unto them, there is no blame on you—and the wives of your sons that are from your loins; and it is forbidden to you to have two sisters together in marriage, except what has already passed; surely, God is Most Forgiving, Ever Merciful. (4:23)

Such vast differences between the two Shari'as [of Adam's and Mohamed's eras], due to the difference in the level of nations, clearly indicate that it would be a gross mistake to assume that the Islamic Shari'a of the seventh century is suitable, in all its details, for application in the twentieth century. The difference between the level of the seventh century and that of the twentieth century is beyond comparison. One need not elaborate upon this self-evident fact. We are then faced with two alternatives. Either Islam as brought by the Prophet and contained in the Qur'an is capable of answering the needs of society in the twentieth century by guiding it in legislation and moral values, or else its capabilities, which have successfully regulated society in the seventh century and the similar societies that followed it, are now exhausted. In this [second] case, humanity of the twentieth century should abandon Islam and seek answers to its problems in other philosophies. This latter alternative cannot be espoused by any Muslim. Nevertheless, Muslims seem unaware of the need to evolve Shari'a. They continue to think that the problems of the twentieth century may be resolved by the same legislation that resolved the problems of the seventh century. This is obviously irrational.

Muslims maintain that the Islamic Shari'a is perfect. This is true, but its perfection consists precisely in the ability to evolve, assimilate the capabilities of individuals and society, and guide such life up the ladder of continuous development, however active, vital, and renewed such social and individual life may be. When Muslims hear us speak of the evolution of Shari'a, they say: "Islamic Shari'a is perfect and does not therefore need to evolve and develop, as only the imperfect evolves and develops." This position is the exact opposite of the truth. It is in fact those who are perfect who evolve and develop. Perfect men aspire to God's description of Himself when He said: "Every day He [reveals Himself] in a fresh state." (55:29) They renew their intellectual and emotional life continuously. The tiny grass that grows at the foot of the mountain, flourishes, blossoms, sheds its seeds on the soil, then withers and is blown away by the wind is more perfect than the mountain which towers over it and endures the wildest storms. The tiny grass is part of an advanced stage of evolution, namely, that of life and death. The mountain has not yet been honored by being part of this process, although it aspires and longs for it.

In the same way, the perfection of the Islamic Shari'a lies in the fact that it is a living body, growing and developing with the living, growing, and developing life, guiding its steps, and charting its way toward God, stage by stage. Life continues on its way back to God, inevitably: "O man,

you are toiling along towards your Lord, and you shall meet Him." (84:6)
This meeting shall take place through the grace of God and the guidance
of the Islamic Shari'a in its three levels: *Shari'a, tariqah,* and *haqiqah.* 8

The evolution of Shari'a, as mentioned above, is simply its evolution
by moving from one text [of the Qur'an] to the other, from a text that is
suitable to govern in the seventh century, and was so implemented, to a
text which was, at the time, too advanced and therefore had to be
abrogated. God said: "Whenever We abrogate any verse or postpone it,9
We bring a better verse, or a similar one. Do you not know that God is
capable of everything?" (2:106) The phrase, "When we abrogate any
verse" means cancel or repeal it, and the phrase "or postpone it" means to
delay its action or implementation. The phrase "We bring a better verse"
means bringing one that is closer to the understanding of the people and
more relevant to their time than the postponed verse; "or a similar one"
means reinstating the same verse when the time comes for its implementation. It is as if the abrogated verses were abrogated in accordance with
the needs of the time, and postponed until their appropriate time comes.
When it does, they become the suitable and operative verses and are
implemented, while those that were implemented in the seventh century
become abrogated. The dictates of the time in the seventh century were
for the subsidiary verses. For the twentieth century they are the primary
verses. This is the rationale of abrogation. . . . [In other words it was not
intended to be] final and conclusive abrogation, but merely postponement
until the appropriate time.

In this evolution we consider the rationale beyond the text. If a
subsidiary verse, which used to overrule the primary verse in the seventh
century, has served its purpose completely and become irrelevant for the
new era, the twentieth century, then the time has come for it to be
abrogated and for the primary verse to be enacted. In this way, the

8. While Shari'a is the law prescribed by God to regulate all aspects of public and
private life, tariqah is the self-imposed and more rigorous worship and guidance practices
adopted by some over and above Shari'a requirements. Haqiqah is the ultimate truth thereby
perceived.

9. The author writes the corresponding Arabic word of the Qur'an as *"nunsi'ha,"* using
the Arabic "hamza," which makes the word mean "postpone," because *nas'a* is delay in
time. Some translators of the Qur'an, such as A. Yusuf Ali, write the word as *"nunsyha"*
which translates as "cause it to be forgotten." The difference in writing the Arabic word,
and its impact on the meaning of the whole verse, is extremely significant to the author's
thesis. Since the implication of the Qur'an being "forgotten," thereby making its text liable
to distortion and misrepresentation, is contrary to fundamental Islamic belief, I am
inclined to accept the author's representation of the Arabic word in the Qur'an.

primary verse has its turn as the operative text in the twentieth century and becomes the basis of the new legislation. This is what the evolution of Shari'a means. It is shifting from one text that served its purpose and was exhausted to another text that was postponed until its time came. Evolution is therefore neither unrealistic or premature, nor expressing a naive and immature opinion. It is merely shifting from one text to the other.

WHO IS AUTHORIZED TO MAKE THE SHIFT?

The Messenger of God passed away, leaving what was abrogated and what was implemented as they were. Is there anyone who is now authorized to make this fundamental change, by implementing what was abrogated and abrogating what was implemented?

In fact, many who oppose our call to the Second Message of Islam do not oppose the substance of our cause; they do not even pay much attention to the substance of this cause. They oppose the form. They object to there being a Message, one requiring a Messenger, who has to be a prophet, since prophethood has been terminated by an express and conclusive text. It is true that prophethood has been terminated, but it is not true that the Message has been terminated: "Mohamed was not the father of any of your men, but the Messenger of God and the seal of the Prophets. . . . God has full knowledge of all things." (33:40)

It is well known that every messenger is a prophet, but not every prophet a messenger. But what is prophethood? Prophethood means that a person is informed by God and informative of God, that is, receiving knowledge from God through revelation, and conveying knowledge from God to people in accordance with what he receives and according to the understanding of the people. By virtue of revelation from God, a man is a prophet, and by virtue of his function as a teacher to people, he becomes a messenger. This is common knowledge. But now we need to examine the reason or rationale for the termination of prophethood in its traditional sense: why was prophethood terminated?

First of all, it must be noted that prophethood was not terminated until all that Heaven wished to reveal to the people of the earth had been revealed and received. This revelation came in stages, according to *hukm al-waqt*, from Adam until Mohamed. This revelation is the Qur'an, and the conclusion of its revelation is the reason why prophethood has been terminated. The rationale behind termination of prophethood is that people should now receive knowledge from God without the intercession of the angel Gabriel; they should receive knowledge from God directly. This may seem strange at first, but it is in fact the self-evident truth. The Qur'an is the literal word of God, and whenever we read it, God is addressing us directly, even though we do not always understand. . . . Why is that? Because we are distracted from Him. As God said: "Nay, but that which they have earned is rust upon their hearts. Nay, they are surely screened from their Lord." (83:14–15). The Qur'an came with its methodology in Shari'a and in *tariqah,* and with the necessary self-discipline to remove the cover (rust) so that we can understand what God is telling us in the Qur'an. A person who achieves such understanding of the Qur'an becomes authorized to speak of its secrets to the extent he understands from God.

WHO IS THE MESSENGER OF THE SECOND MESSAGE?

He is one to whom God granted understanding from the Qur'an and authorized to speak.

HOW DO WE KNOW HIM?

It has been reported that Jesus said to his disciples: "Beware the false prophets!" They said: "How do we know them?" He replied: "You shall know them by their fruits."

Introduction to the Third Edition

This is the introduction to the third edition of *The Second Message of Islam*. The first edition was published in January 1967, in the revered month of Ramadan, 1386 (A.H.). The second edition was published in April 1968, in the month of Muharam 1388 (A.H.). At the time of the second edition we were, however, preoccupied with other business and could not give that edition an introduction of its own.

This book, *The Second Message of Islam,* is new in every respect. . . . Besides being new, it is also totally "strange," that is, unexpected, since it proclaims the return of a renewed Islam. Such "strangeness," however, is to be expected, especially by informed Muslims. The Prophet is reported to have said: "Islam started as a stranger, and it shall return as a stranger in the same way it started. Blessed are the strangers! They asked: Who are the strangers, Oh Messenger of God? He replied: Those who revive my Sunnah after it had been abandoned."

Thus, the return of a revived Islam is by nature strange, that is to say, mysterious and unexpected. Those who criticize this book for its "strangeness," therefore, reveal both a lack of understanding and of patience. We need not concern ourselves here with those who oppose this book's message out of misunderstanding and deliberate distortion out of bad faith. But we must emphasize that the apparent "strangeness" of this message is inherent in the nature of Islamic revival. Understanding this book requires patience, diligence, and close scrutiny. If the reader is able to persist, his mind shall be open to a new understanding of the Qur'an and Islam, and he shall be rewarded for his perseverance, God willing.

SUNNAH AND SHARI'A

In the above quoted Hadith, the Prophet referred to the strangers and
said they were those who revive his Sunnah after it had been abandoned.
Those who call for such a revival become strangers amongst their own
people, because such a call involves a divergence from what people are
accustomed to. They are strangers by virtue of their adherence to the
truth amongst people for whom the truth is a stranger. If people have
experienced falsehood for so long, then because of their long unfamiliarity
with the truth, they come to accept falsehood as the truth.

It is mistakenly believed by some that the Sunnah consists of all the
acts and words of the Prophet, as well as his approval of the action of
others. This is not true, because his teachings to others and approval of
their conduct relate to Shari'a. Only the Prophet's personal deeds, and his
utterances that reflect the state of his heart in its knowledge of God,
constitute Sunnah. The Prophet's statements which were designed to
teach the people their religion are Shari'a. The difference between
Shari'a and Sunnah is the difference between the Message and the
Prophethood. In other words, it reflects the difference between the
standard of the generality of Muslims of all levels, and the standard of the
Prophet, which is a tremendous difference indeed.

Sunnah relates to the personal practice of the Prophet, while in
Shari'a the Prophet descends from the level of his own personal practice
to the level of his people in order to teach them according to their
capabilities, thereby requiring them to act within their capacities. Sunnah is his prophethood, while Shari'a is his message. With respect to his
message, the Prophet said: "We the prophets have been instructed to
address people in accordance with the level of their understanding."

AL-ISLAM AND AL-IMAN

There is a common failure to appreciate the fine distinction between
al-islam and al-iman. Al-iman is widely and mistakenly believed to be
superior to al-islam. This mistaken belief is due to an inability to appreciate the circumstances of the time. The time when such belief sufficed is
over, as we have now reached a point when the understanding of religion
has developed and evolved from the level of al-iman to the level of al-
islam. The distinction can be explained as follows:

Al-islam is an intellectual process by which the diligent worshiper proceeds on a ladder of seven steps, the first being *al-islam*, secondly *al-iman*, thirdly *al-ihsan*, fourthly *'ilm al-yaqin*, fifthly *'ilm 'ayn al-yaqin*, sixthly *'ilm haqq al-yaqin*, and seventhly *al-islam* once more.[1] But *al-islam* at the higher stage differs in degree from *al-islam* at the initial stage. At the initial stage, *al-islam* is merely external or apparent submission, while in the final state it is both external and internal (genuine) submission. *Al-islam* at the initial stage concerns speech and action, while in the final stage it is intelligent surrender and submission and acceptance of God both in private and in public. At the initial stage *al-islam* is inferior to *al-iman*, while at the final stage it is superior to *al-iman*. Many theologians whom we know today are unable to make this distinction.

Religious scholars have been confused by the Hadith involving Gabriel, reported by 'Umar ibn al-Khatab, who said:

As we were seated with the Messenger of God, peace be upon him, there came a man wearing [clean] white clothes, with very dark hair. None of us knew him, yet he did not show the signs of travel. He sat near the Messenger of God, peace be upon him, and placed his knees next to his [the Prophet's] knees, and placed his hands on his [the Prophet's] thighs and said: Oh, Mohamed, tell me about *al-islam*. . . . He [the Prophet] said: *Al-islam* is to declare that there is no god but God, and that Mohamed is the Messenger of God; to say the prayers; pay *al-zakat*; fast the month, and do pilgrimage to the House [of God], if you can afford it.[2] He said: You are right. We wondered how he could ask him and then confirm he was right. Then he [the man] said: Tell me about *al-iman*. He (the Prophet) replied: *Al-iman* is to believe in God, His angels, His Books, Messengers, fate whether good or bad, and the hereafter. He [the man] said: you are right. Then he asked: tell me about *al-ihsan*. He [the Prophet] replied: *Al-ihsan* is to worship God as if you see Him, and although you do not see Him, be certain that He can see you. He [the man] said: you are right. Then he said: Tell me when is the final hour? He [the Prophet] replied: the one being asked does not know of it more than the one who asks. He [the man] said: Tell me of its signs? He [the Prophet] replied: When the woman gives birth to her

1. These somewhat technical terms refer to the various degrees of piety and perfection of conduct and lifestyle, in accordance with religious and moral norms and ethics.
2. Payment of the prescribed alms, fasting the days of the month of Ramadan, and making a pilgrimage to Mecca once in a lifetime, together with the five daily prayers and affirmation of the faith are the duty of every Muslim.

mistress, and when you see the bare-footed and naked shepherds practice extravagance. He said: You are right. Then he left. We stayed a
while, then the Messenger, peace be upon him, said: Oh Omar, do you
know the one who was asking the questions? I replied, God and His
Messenger know better. He said: This is Gabriel, who came to teach you
your religion.

Many religious scholars interpreted this to mean that Islam proceeds
in three stages: al-islam, al-iman, and al-ihsan. Since it is said in the
Qur'an, concerning the Bedouins "The Bedouins said amanna [we be-
lieve]; tell them you have not believed, but say aslamna [we submit] and al-
iman [true belief] did not enter your hearts yet" (49:14), it seems obvious
to these scholars that al-iman is higher in degree than al-islam. Those
scholars failed to appreciate that the issue needs close consideration.

THE TRUTH OF THE MATTER

The truth of the matter is that al-islam, as conveyed in the Qur'an,
comes in two stages: the stage of dogma (al-'aqidah) and the stage of the
truth (al-haqiqah) or knowledge. Each of these two stages has three levels.
The levels of dogma are al-islam, al-iman, and al-ihsan, while the
levels of knowledge are "ilm al-yaqin, 'ilm 'ayn al-yaqin, and 'ilm haqq al-
yaqin. Finally, there is a seventh stage in the ladder of evolution, which is
al-islam, which completes the cycle. The end of religious evolution
resembles the beginning, yet they are not identical. The beginning is al-
islam and the end is al-islam, but there is a vast difference between al-islam
at the beginning of religious evolution and al-islam at the end. The stage
of al-'aqidah is the stage of the nation of Mu'minin, which is the nation of
the First Message Of Islam.
The stage of knowledge is the stage of the nation of Muslimin, which
is the nation of the Second Message of Islam. This nation has not come
yet, although its vanguard have appeared individually throughout human
history, in the form of prophets, with the final prophet being the Prophet
Mohamed ibn Abdullahi, may he receive the highest blessing and utmost
peace. It was Mohamed who prophesied the coming of the nation of
Muslimin and brought its message, as contained in general terms in the
Qur'an, and detailed it in the Sunnah. When the nation of Muslimin
comes, it shall begin at the same point as the nation of Mu'minin, namely
at a stage of dogma or al-'aqidah. But it shall not stop at the third step of

the ladder, where Gabriel stopped in his questions. It shall continue to evolve to the end of the ladder, thereby combining both dogma as well as knowledge. In other words, the coming nation is a nation of both Muslimin as well as Mu'minin at one and the same time, while the first nation was one of Mu'minin (believers) and not Muslimin (submitters) in the final sense of *al-islam* [as total and intelligent surrender to God].

It must be noted that Gabriel stopped in his questions at the end of the level of dogma, *al-'aqidah*, because he had come to explain religion to the nation of Mu'minin, and not to the nation of Muslimin, which had not yet come.

Mohamed is the Messenger of the First Message, and he is also the Messenger of the Second Message. While he explained the First Message in detail, he only outlined the Second Message. Its elaboration now requires a fresh understanding of the Qur'an. That is the purpose of this book.

Those who approach this book with an open mind will be guided along the right path. We ask God for rectification and success in our endeavor; He is the best Lord.

Preface

"Today I have perfected your religion for you, completed My grace upon you, and sanctioned Islam as your faith." (5:3)

When the divine word was proclaimed through the illiterate Mohamed, in the hills of Mecca in the seventh century A.D., a new civilization emerged to raise human worth to a peak unprecedented in human history. Building on the ruins of the material civilization of the Persian civilization in the East, this new civilization received its ultimate articulation, at least from the theoretical point of view, when God revealed to his Prophet the verse quoted above: "Today I have perfected your religion for your benefit, and completed My grace upon you, and sanctioned Islam as your faith."

That was the end of the first third of the seventh century. When the Prophet passed away soon after, the new civilization lost momentum. As one of the companions put it: "No sooner had we dusted from our hands the soil of the Messenger of God's grave than we disowned our hearts."[1] In fact, as early as the end of the reign of the third *Khalifa* Osman [end of the second decade after the Prophet's death], during the period known in Islamic history as *al-fitnah al-kubra* [the Great Upheavel], this statement proved to be only too true.

From that point onwards, Islamic civilization continued to decline, although the base of Islam broadened, embracing much of the Roman and

---

1. That is, the early Muslims felt that their faith was shaken and their commitment to the Islamic way of life diminished, immediately upon the death of the Prophet.

Persian civilizations upon whose very ruins, as we have stated, Islam initially arose. It is true that history repeats itself, but it does not do so in the same manner, because events often recur in ways that are in some ways similar but in other ways dissimilar to former events. Place is not spherical, nor, consequently, is time. Indeed, both are helical, proceeding from the bottom to the top where the end of the cycle resembles its beginning, yet it is also different.

In the same way that time, on this planet of ours, proceeds on two feet, those of night and day, darkness and light, and in the same way that man walks on two feet, left and right, so life progresses on two feet, material and spiritual. When human society, in its development, advances the material foot, puts it down, and leans upon it, it would be ready to advance the spiritual foot, as it is bound to do so: "that is an absolute imperative of your Lord." (19:71) In other words, the progress of life neither halts, nor delays, nor repeats itself. It proceeds forward in its development because life strives to be perfect in form, as it is perfect in essence, although that objective shall never be exhaustively achieved.

It may also be said that the progress of human civilization is like that of a wave, always between a trough and a crest. When it is at the bottom of the trough, it is only gaining momentum in order to climb to the crest. The hollow represents the material progress of human society, while the crest represents its spiritual peak. Material progress is often disdained as the corrupt work of Satan by those who are unable to see the full picture of social development. [They fail to appreciate that] God is drawing life towards Him, on both these two feet of matter and spirit. In fact, from the point of view of monotheism (tawhid), matter and spirit are one thing, not differing in kind, but only in degree.

1

Civilization and Material Progress

Civilization is different from material progress, but it is a difference in degree and not in kind. Civilization is the peak of human development, while material progress is its base.

Civilization may be defined as the ability to distinguish values and to observe these values in daily conduct. A civilized man does not confuse ends with means, and he does not sacrifice ends for the sake of means. He is a man of principles and of moral values, one who has achieved a complete intellectual and emotional life.

IS CIVILIZATION MORALITY?

Yes, it most certainly is! But what is morality? In our view, the best definition of morality is discretion in the exercise of absolute individual freedom. The Prophet said: "I have been sent to perfect the highest moral values." It is as if he said I have been sent for the sole purpose of perfecting the highest moral values. That is why we said earlier that Mohamed was the ultimate articulation of the civilization brought by God through him. God described him by saying: "You are of great moral character." (68:4) When Aisha, the Prophet's wife, was asked about the Prophet's moral values, she said: "His moral values were the Qur'an." It is known that the Qur'an is the morals of God.[1] God's morals are in

1. The Qur'an, being the speech of God, is infinitely more than the text conveyed in the Arabic language, and the Qur'an is ultimately of God Himself, infinite in every moral value.

infinitude, *itlaq,* hence the definition that morality is discretion in the exercise of absolute individual freedom. Mohamed was the most able of all men in exercising this discretion, in his strict regard for his Lord as well as his own self-discipline, in whatever he did or left undone, with regard to God and with regard to others. Is it not he who said: "Hold yourselves to account before you are held to account"?

In fact, the Sunnah of the Prophet is the ultimate expression of discretion in the exercise of absolute individual freedom. It was to this Sunnah that the Prophet was referring in his well-known Hadith where he says: "Islam started as a stranger, and it shall return as a stranger in the same way it started. Blessed are the strangers! They asked: Who are the strangers, O Messenger of God? He replied: Those who revive my Sunnah after it had been abandoned." The Prophet's Sunnah demonstrated his ability, in his everyday life, to show discretion in exercising his absolute individual freedom. The Sunnah, thus, is the peak of moral values, reflecting the peak of human civilization.

Material progress, on the other hand, means the enjoyment of certain comforts and benefits of an advanced standard of living. Thus, if a man owns a grand car, a beautiful house, and nice furniture, he enjoys material progress. If he obtained these means at the expense of his freedom, then he is not civilized, even though he is materially advanced. It is thus possible for a person to enjoy material progress without being civilized, or be civilized without enjoying the comforts of material progress. While the first phenomenon is quite common, the second is rare. We strive today to achieve both material progress and civilization at one and the same time.

WESTERN CIVILIZATION

According to the above definitions, present-day Western civilization is not a civilization at all, despite all its material progress. It is not a civilization because its values are confused, in that means are advanced while ends are retarded. In our book *Risalat al-Salah* (A Treatise on Prayer) we said: "The present industrialized Western civilization is a two-faced coin . . . a bright and brilliant face and an ugly one. . . . The bright face is its scientific and material advancements, and the capacity to employ these achievements to improve human life. Its ugly face, on the other hand, is the failure to intelligently pursue peace. This failure forces it to prepare for war and spend on the means of destruction many times the amount of money and energy that it does for peace and development.

Another failure in industrialized Western civilization has been its inability to reconcile the needs of the individual with the needs of the community, that is, the need of the individual for absolute individual freedom and the need of the community for total social justice. In fact, the failure to reconcile these two needs has bedeviled human progress throughout history.

This failure is proof of the inadequacy of philosophies and ideologies throughout history to the present day. It is precisely in this respect, the reconciliation of individual freedom with the community's need for social justice, that Islam has the clearest advantage over other philosophies and ideologies."[2]

The confusion of values in materialistic Western civilization indicated in the above quotation from *Risalat al-Salah* is clearly reflected in the emphasis placed by Russian Communism on society, which is in fact the means, rather than on the individual, who is the end. Western capitalism is not, in this respect, in any way better than Russian communism.[3]

FAILURE OF WESTERN CIVILIZATION

This present-day industrialized Western civilization has reached the end of its development. It has obviously failed to answer the needs of modern human society. Post-World War II society lacks the stability enjoyed by the post-World War I society. The victor in the First World War was also the victor in peace, and as such it was able to regulate the international community. In one way or another, and whatever may have been its defects, it was able to achieve disarmament to such an extent and long enough to achieve a degree of stability. The apparent victor in the Second World War, namely Britain, was vanquished in the peace that followed. But strictly speaking, there was no victor and no vanquished after the Second World War. All were in the same boat, wrapped under the black wing of perplexity. Now, over twenty years have elapsed since the end of the war,[4] and yet humanity is still in a state of war because of fear of war. We speak of peace, yet we spend on armaments many times what we spend on development, because the only way we know for

2. *Risalat al-Salah*, 7th edition, pp. 55–56 (Arabic).
3. As indicated by this paragraph, the author perceives Western civilization as including both the Marxist as well as the capitalist liberal traditions. See chapter 2.
4. This book was written in 1966; its first edition appeared in January 1967.

maintaining peace is to threaten each other with the consequences of starting a war.

The reason behind the failure of the present industrialized Western civilization to answer the needs of contemporary society is that it has reached the end of its purely material development. It now awaits the introduction of a new element to supplement and revive its lost vigor, thereby increasing its potential for development and its ability to follow up and guide the activity of modern society. Russia, for instance, now facing failure in achieving socialism, let alone communism, retreats and adopts measures more akin to capitalism than socialism, seeking thereby to provide new incentives for production. This clearly illustrates the fact that the present Western civilization has reached the end of its purely material development and finds itself at the end of a dead-end street. It will have to go back to the crossroads and adopt a different route from the one it took half a century ago in the excitement and excessive zeal of revolution. Chinese communism, which came late on the scene, will soon find time running out as the large gap between the potential of modern human society and the inadequacy of Western civilization becomes clearer every day. When confronted with this awful contradiction, China sought to relieve it through that hysterical condition which it ironically called the Cultural Revolution, conducted by adolescents in the streets and public places against scientists and university professors. It also sought the deification of Mao Tse-tung, making his writings the only source of culture and wisdom, as if they were the ultimate in intellectual activity.

There is no need to dwell on the capitalist West in this context, because the contradictions of Western civilization are represented by communism in Russia and China more than in the West. Moreover, the capitalist West is not offering a new theory for Western civilization. Capitalism is only attempting to maintain its traditional position (except for a slight development prompted by the extremism of the Communist Revolution, which forced the West to meet it halfway), in order to preserve its own traditional order in the face of this sweeping revolution.

This failure of the present industrialized Western civilization is therefore due to the fact that its material development was not supplemented by proper moral growth that clarifies the confusion and places the machine in its proper place as the servant of man and not his master. Material progress has unfortunately not been shored up by spiritual progress. In current social thinking, as stated above, bread is valued more than liberty. This is true today of socialism as well as capitalism.

In fact, communism differs from capitalism only in degree. It is in essence as materialistic as capitalism, albeit more efficient in achieving fairer distribution. The apparent enmity between the two ideologies is similar to disagreements between various sects of the same religion, reflecting unity of their foundation rather than difference of origin.

In summary, the reason for the failure of industrialized Western civilization is its inability to answer two questions: What is the nature of the relationship between the individual and the community? And what is the nature of the relationship between the individual and the universe?

2

Philosophy's View of the Individual and the Community

Social philosophy throughout the ages, up to and including contemporary communism, has failed to appreciate the relationship between the individual and the community. It was assumed if the individual found the opportunity to exercise his freedom, his activity would go against the interest of the community. As the community was considered to be greater than the individual, then its interest deserved to be put before those of the individual. Hence, the freedom of the individual was curtailed in the interest of the community whenever it appeared that the two were inconsistent.

In fact, throughout history, the freedom of the individual has often been at odds with the interest of the community. It would even appear that the community was always organized and safeguarded by placing limitations upon individual freedom. As the human individual was rising from a savage state, in which he was concerned with nothing except seeking to satisfy his physical and sexual needs, and because human society, in its initial stages, could not have begun until man's desires were curtailed, there evolved customs regulating sexual relations. They prohibited sex between brother and sister, father and daughter, mother and son, father and son's wife, and son and his father's wife, even before the prohibition of adultery in general. These prohibitions, that is to say the first laws, helped to curb sexual jealousy, which used to divide the human family whenever the sons reached manhood. It became possible, once these customs were established, for father, adult son, son-in-law, and married son, to live in the same house or neighboring houses, with each of them feeling that his wife was safe from the others. It may be that

56

customs regulating individual ownership evolved at the same time. In primitive societies there was not much difference between ownership of wives, tools, or caves. As it was essential for small communities to live in harmony in the same place and in ever increasing numbers, hunting, fighting enemies, and overcoming daily hardships united, it was imperative to adopt limitations in order to regulate conduct in the community and preserve its integrity. The death penalty was executed against every individual found guilty of adultery within the above indicated circles, whether a man or a woman. The death penalty was also imposed on individuals who stole from close relatives and was later applied to thieves in general, as communities became larger. The penalty was subsequently reduced to amputation, depriving a thief of a limb instead of his life. As individuals evolved in refinement and intelligence, they were deterred by less drastic measures than their ancestors.

This does not mean that all societies began in the same manner, but they all, no doubt, started around similar customs, traditions, and laws that made human society itself possible.

As early individuals were so savage, cruel, insensitive, and animal-like, extreme violence was required to tame and transform them from savagery to sociability. Hence, early social custom had to be severe and violent, frequently imposing the death penalty for minor violations. Often innocent individuals had to sacrifice their lives in the service of their community. Human sacrifices were performed in the temples in order to bring upon the community the blessing of the gods, or to appease the gods' anger when they were thought to be angry. Such customs, forfeiting the freedom of the individual for the well-being of the community, were widely practiced until relatively recent times.

Even during the time of the Prophet Abraham, the father of prophets, who lived about two thousand years before the birth of Christ, human sacrifice was logically and religiously acceptable. Abraham himself was ordered to slaughter his son Isma'il and was about to obey the order, without fear or hesitation, when God granted the abrogation of the law. At that point, the custom was repealed and human sacrifice was replaced by sacrifice of an inferior animal, thereby enhancing the promotion of man above animal. God tells us about Abraham and Isma'il:

And Abraham said, "I am going to my Lord, who shall guide me." He prayed: "My Lord, grant me a righteous son." So We promised him an intelligent son. When the boy was old enough to accompany his father,

Abraham told him, "Oh, son, I see in my dream that I should offer you in sacrifice, so consider this and tell me what you think." The boy replied, "Oh father, do as you are commanded and you shall find me, if God please, steadfast in my faith." When they both were ready to submit to the will of God and Abraham placed his son for slaughter, We called upon him: Oh Abraham: you have already fulfilled the dream. Thus do We reward those who do good. This, surely, was a manifest trial. We ransomed the boy with a great sacrifice. And we left this blessing for subsequent generations. Peace be upon Abraham. (37:99–108)

"And we left this blessing, etc." means, among other things, the abrogation of the law according to which human individuals were sacrificed. It was, however, through the practice of that law through the ages that man evolved and was elevated from his previous beastly existence, hence becoming worthy of being ransomed by offering an inferior beast in his place.

This is the case now, notwithstanding the current forms of violence to which an individual is subjected, which are bound to disappear as opportunities for enlightenment and maturity increase. Human sacrifice did not end at the stroke of a pen at the time of the Prophet Abraham, however. History tells us that when the Muslims conquered Egypt, they found human sacrifice still practiced in the custom of the "Nile's Bride." It is reported that 'Amru ibn al-'As, conqueror of Egypt and its ruler at the time, was attracted one day by great excitement. When he inquired, he was told that the people had the custom of selecting one of the most beautiful girls from the best of families, so as to celebrate throwing her into the Nile, every year, in order to spare her people from drought, as she would tempt the Nile to flood them with good omens and prosperity. 'Amru ibn al-'As then requested that they should delay the giving of the bride until he asked for instructions from 'Umar ibn al-Khatab [the Khalifa or ruler of all Muslims] on the matter. He wrote to 'Umar who responded with his well-known reply:

In the name of God the Merciful and Compassionate from the slave of God 'Umar ibn al-Khatab, the Prince of the Believers, to the Nile of Egypt. Peace be upon you, together with the mercy of God and His grace.

Now, if you flood of your own accord, then do not flood. But if you flood from God, then do.

'Umar asked 'Amru to throw the letter into the Nile, and he did. The Nile flooded and the custom was abandoned from that date. In this way, religious knowledge once again saved the human individual.

Thus, since the dawn of history, and certainly long before, human sacrifice and other forms of personal violence have been used, until recent times, as we have shown in the above two examples. Philosophers were misled by this historical experience into believing that freedom for the individual is necessarily incompatible with the interest of the community. They then concluded that it is only rational to sacrifice the freedom of the individual for the sake of the interest of the community. Now communism, the leading contemporary social philosophy, playing the role of the progressive and intelligent ideology in the current industrialized Western civilization, has fallen prey to the same fallacy.

PHILOSOPHICAL THINKING ON THE INDIVIDUAL AND THE UNIVERSE

The relationship between man and the universe is even more misunderstood than the relationship between the individual and the community. This is less apparent because the relationship between the individual and the community has required practical and urgent consideration in politics, legislation, and social life. The relationship between the individual and the universe, on the other hand, has remained largely in the realm of theory. We are still subject to the animal "herd instinct," not yet intellectually mature enough to step into the realm of individuality. But there are increasingly signs that the age of the collectivity is giving way to the age of individuality. This age of individuality shall dawn when the fallacy of the alleged conflict between the individual and the community is resolved in theory and then in practice. This is a subject which we shall discuss in detail, God willing.

The relationship between the individual and the universe is not only a question of theoretical philosophy to be relegated to the realm of idle contemplation. It is an urgent concern upon which depend both the achievement of individuality and the effective functioning of the community in order to make it capable of producing individuals who may be expected to achieve their individuality.

The failure of social philosophy to understand properly the relationship between the individual and the universe has been apparent in human experience since prehistoric times. When early man stood on his two feet for the first time and intelligently faced the natural environment in which he lived, he found it teeming with tremendous forces, alien to his nature, hostile to his wishes, and often uncontrollable. Early man perceived these forces as not only indifferent but, in many cases, actively seeking to destroy his very existence. Those tremendous primitive natural forces which shared the earth with primitive man could be classified as either hunter or hunted—beasts were hunted while they hunted others, and the hunters who hunted were themselves hunted. It was as if the whole environment was in constant struggle for survival, and man himself had to learn caution and trickery to preserve his own life.

Many forces, both harmful and beneficial, encountered by primitive man could not be combated or outwitted. So man tried to appease or supplicate these natural forces. Thus he humbled himself, and gave presents and sacrifices, and practiced worship and rituals. On the other hand, there were forces of the natural environment which he could overcome, so he adopted various tricks. Early man built houses in trees, on mountaintops, and on poles made from tree trunks and placed in water and other inaccessible places. He also expanded his fighting ability by constructing weapons from trees and stone.

Between worship and combat, man felt lonely and anxious as the only creature of his kind, surrounded by enemies who lurked, waiting to take him by surprise. All this led man to believe that the universe was a world of enmity and hostility.

Philosophy has concluded that religion of all kinds and up to the present, is nothing but a symptom of humanity's childhood, whereby early man appealed to an imaginary god to satisfy his need for a protecting father. It was assumed that the rule of the environment was struggle not appeasement, and that man was forced to appease only when unable to fight successfully. According to that approach, man's progress from early stone weapons to the present stage of the hydrogen bomb has made his dependence on religion superfluous, because his ability to combat has been perfected, or almost perfected. Consequently, [it is maintained that] man should abandon religious feeling, religion, and even God.

Khrushchev is alleged to have said that when [cosmonaut Yuri] Gagarine circled outer space for the first time, he did not find the creature they call God. It is as if Khrushchev could not imagine God except of the same matter which he claims to know. Thus, since communist ideology is unable to envision anything beyond matter, it converts its failure into a virtue and denies the existence of anything beyond matter. Communism made this claim in order to maintain that man, as he struggles with his material environment, develops in understanding it, and improves his means of struggle, until he conquers and manipulates it, thereby becoming the master of his own fate.

Man's relationship to the universe has never been more misunderstood than with communism, and in the name of science and philosophy. Yet communism is the leading contemporary social philosophy, playing the role of the progressive and intelligent ideology in the current industrialized Western civilization. Is the Christian West different from the communist East with respect to religion and God?

There may be difference from the traditional theological point of view, but not from the practical point of view. There is nothing in the West's conception of religion and God which restrains it from becoming Communist. Russia, before the Communist revolution, was Christian, and even Orthodox Christian.

In fact, all religion today, whether Christianity or Islam, must face the challenge of relevance to modern society, as well as to its individual members. Religion must answer all the needs of individual and community life in an intelligent and rational way, or else it will become irrelevant in the real life of the people and diminish in influence. It will be replaced by another philosophy, however erroneous it may be, so long as such philosophy appears to be capable of providing practical answers for daily problems and serves the people's material interests, if only in the short run. As long as people have physical needs, calls to virtue should not disregard those needs. In fact, it is in the nature of things that people should be invited to virtue through the satisfaction of their physical needs.

Notwithstanding the apparent differences between the communist East and the Christian West, present industrialized Western civilization is not truly Christian. It has failed to understand the relationship between the individual and the community, or between the individual and the universe. Because of these failures, Western civilization is unable to combine socialism with democracy in practice. This is the clearest demonstration of its inadequacy.

We are not concerned here with deprecating Western civilization or belittling it, but rather wish to study it scientifically and put it in its proper place. We wish to acknowledge its advantages and advocate its reform so that it evolves into a true civilization rather than remaining satisfied with its material progress.

3

The Individual and Community in Islam

The first thing to note is that in Islam the individual is the end. Everything else, including the Qur'an and the religion of Islam itself, are means to that end. Women are fully equal to men in this respect. This means that the human being, whether man or woman, sane or insane, should never be used as a means to another end, as he or she is the end to which all means should lead.

This individuality is the essence of the whole endeavor, as it is the basis of responsibility and honor. When the scales of reckoning are set, they are set for the individual, whether a man or a woman. This is a point we wish to emphasize. God says: "Nor does any bearer of burden bear the burden of another" (6:164); "Then whoso does an atom's weight of good will see it. And whoso does an atom's weight of evil will also see it" (99:7–8); "And We shall inherit him and all that he said, and he shall come to Us all alone" (19:80); "Everybody in heaven and the earth shall come to the Gracious [God] as a slave. He comprehends them [by His knowledge] and has numbered them all fully. And each of them shall come to Him, on the Day of Resurrection, all alone" (19:93–95); and "And [now] you have come to Us as individuals in the same way we have created you in the first place" (6:94).

This equality between men and women is the universal rule of Islam, and Shari'a law discriminated between the two only because of circumstances prevailing at the various stages of development of society.

In Islam significance is attributed to an individual to the degree of his knowledge of God. Islam has made every individual an end to himself, even the mentally retarded, because everyone is the germ of an individual who is knowledgeable of God, and he shall achieve such knowledge sooner or later. "That is an absolute imperative of your Lord." (19:71)

At the beginning of this book we asserted that Islam was able to resolve the apparent conflict between the needs of the individual and the needs of the community, and provide a system in which the needs of the individual for absolute individual freedom become an extension of the needs of the community for total social justice. In other words, Islam succeeded in making the organization of the community a vehicle for freedom. This equilibrium is derived from the concept of monotheism (*tawhid*) that divided Islamic Shari'a into two levels: the level of the community, and the level of the individual. Shari'a at the community level is known as the law of social transactions (*mu'amalat*), while Shari'a at the individual level is known as the law of worship practices (*'ibadat*).

The dominant feature of *mu'amalat* is that it regulates the relationship between one individual and another in the community, while the dominant feature of *'ibadat* is that it regulates the relationship between the individual and the Lord. This does not mean that each of these two sets of laws exists in isolation from the other, but rather that they are two aspects of the same body of law, which exists by virtue of both sets supplementing one another. Moreover, these two sets of laws differ from each other only in degree and not in essence. That is to say, *mu'amalat* is *'ibadat* at a crude level, while *'ibadat* is *mu'amalat* at a superior level. This is because individuality is more pronounced in *'ibadat*, worship, than *mu'amalat*, social transactions.

It is clear, however, that worship has no value unless it is reflected in one's relations with the community in a way which is worship practice in itself. The Prophet described the whole of religion as being *mu'amalat* by saying: "Religion is how you deal with others." In other words, worship in private represents a school in which the individual receives theoretical preparation, with the opportunity for practical implementation through living in the community and dealing with others. Monotheism (*tawhid*) asserts that the whole universe has one source, one path, and one destiny. The universe emanates from God, and to God it shall return, but as individuals. "And [now] you have come to Us as individuals in the same way We have created you in the first place." (6:94) Return to God is not achieved by covering distances, but rather through developing qualities resembling God's qualities—that is to say, by bringing the qualities of the limited closer to the qualities of the Infinite.[1] The return of the individual

1. Human beings have a limited and confused image of the qualities of God: life, knowledge, willpower, ability, hearing, sight, and speech. Through consistent enhance-

to God shall be through appropriate means, including Islam, the Qur'an, and the community.

The community has its freedom, which represents the base of the pyramid, while the freedom of the individual represents its peak. In other words, the freedom of the community is the tree, while the freedom of the individual is the fruit. Through this comprehensive perspective, Islam finds no conflict or inconsistency between the individual and the community.

Since Islam achieved this fine balance between the individual and the community through monotheism (*tawhid*), it enacted all its laws in such a way as to reconcile, in the same system, the needs of the individual and the needs of the community. Thus, it neither sacrifices the individual for the sake of the community, which would have defeated the end by the means, nor does it sacrifice the community for the sake of the individual, thereby losing the most important means of achieving individuality. Thus, Islamic law, in all its features, reflects this admirable reconciliation of the needs of the individual for absolute individual freedom with the needs of the community for total social justice.

ABSOLUTE INDIVIDUAL FREEDOM

Many philosophers regard discussion of absolute individual freedom as a fruitless exercise, holding that freedom of the individual must be limited or lead to anarchy. But Islam regards freedom as absolute in essence, and when we speak of freedom, of whatever kind and at whatever level, we speak of an absolute value. Limited freedom is only a hint of infinitude (*itlaq*) being diffused to people on earth in portions they are able to endure. Thus, limitation is not the fundamental quality of freedom. Rather, it is the absolute which is freedom's true essence. Limitation is a transitional requirement related to the development of the individual from the limited to the infinite or absolute.

Thus, freedom in Islam is absolute: every individual has the right to achieve it, regardless of religion or race. But it is a right which corresponds to a duty and must be earned through proper use, namely, discretion in the exercise of freedom. Freedom does not become limited except when the free person is unable to properly discharge his [or her]

---

ment and promotion of his or her limited version of these qualities, making them increasingly resemble those of God, every individual person approaches his or her own meeting with God.

duty, whereby he [or she] must forfeit his [or her] freedom to the extent of his [or her] failure.[2] In such a situation, freedom is limited through laws that are consistent with the constitution, that is to say, laws that are capable of reconciling the needs of the community for total social justice with the needs of the individual for absolute individual freedom. These laws neither sacrifice the individual for the sake of the community, nor sacrifice the community for the sake of the individual, but maintain the proper balance between the two. When implemented, such laws achieve, in one system and at every level of their application, the interest of the individual and the interest of the community.

The absolute [or infinite] is the fundamental quality in Islam, because Islam considers the individual capable of limitless development. He proceeds from the limited to the absolute, from imperfection to perfection, that is to say absolute perfection. The goal of the slave in Islam is to achieve the perfection of God, and the perfection of God is infinite.[3] God says: "Man has nothing except his own achievement. What he achieves he shall meet. Then he shall receive the fullest payment. And to your Lord is the ultimate goal." (53:39–42) This means that God is the purpose of the whole endeavor. As stated above, progress to God is not through traveling distances but rather through the longing of the slave to achieve the qualities of the God. God says: "Oh man, you are toiling along towards your Lord and you shall meet Him" (84:6), whether you want to meet Him or not. And where shall this meeting be? Is it on earth or in heaven? God said: "I am neither contained in my earth nor in my heavens, but rather contained in the heart of my true slave."[4] Thus one meets Him within one's self and such meeting shall be achieved by Him and not by the individual human being.

To this effect the Prophet said: "Adopt the qualities of God, my Lord is on the straight path." God also says: "Be of the Lord because you teach the Book and because you study [it]." (3:39)

2. Gender neutral language is used here to remind the reader that the author perceives men and women as equal. Failure to use gender neutral language in any part of this translation should not, therefore, be seen as implying otherwise.

3. The slave of God is one who is free from all other bondage, i.e., attachment, or at least diligently strives to be so free.

4. This is a Divine Hadith (Hadith qudsi), one of that class of Islamic texts where the Prophet used his own language to express a Divine meaning. It is distinguished from the Qur'an in that the words are not Divine revelation as such, and distinguished from regular Hadith in that their meaning is Divine. In other words, the Qur'an is literally the word of God, regular Hadith is the meaning and words of the Prophet, while Hadith qudsi is Divine meaning expressed in the Prophet's words.

What prevents us from discharging the duty of absolute individual freedom is ignorance; for we are so ignorant that we love our ignorance and hate knowledge unless it comes in a way consistent with our whim. The Qur'an says: "Fighting is ordained to you, though it is repugnant to you, but it may be that you dislike a thing while it is good for you, and it may be that you like a thing while it is bad for you. God Knows and you do not know." (2:216) "[I]t may be that you like a thing while it is bad for you" refers to our selfishness, for we love ourselves, and we love all our follies. Every human being is necessarily and by his very nature selfish. His perfection is, in fact, inherent in that very selfish nature.

The selfishness of every selfish being is of two levels: a lower ignorant selfishness, and a higher intelligent one. The ignorantly selfish being may see his interest in things that are inconsistent with the interest of the community, in order to achieve what he believes to be his own interest. The intelligently selfish being, on the other hand, does not see his interest except as consistent with the interest of others. Thus, he adopts the attitude described by the poet Abu al-'La' al-Ma'rri: "Even if I am granted eternal life, I would not like to have it alone. May there be no rain on me or my land, unless it rains all over the country too."

This meaning is expressed in the revealing statement of the Prophet: "One does not become a believer (mu'min) unless he wishes for his brother what he would wish for himself." In this way, Islam arrays itself against ignorant selfishness, and in support of intelligent selfishness: "One is not a believer," says the Prophet, "unless his wishes are in accordance with what has been revealed to me." Wishes refer to ignorant selfishness. "The worst of your enemies is yourself, which is within your being"—that is, your lower self as opposed to your other superior self, to which the pronoun "your" refers in the phrase "your worst enemy." In other words, the worst enemy of the other superior self is your lower inferior self. Indeed the Qur'an often uses expressions with the two words, "inferior" and "other."[5]

These terms refer to ignorant selfishness, as opposed to intelligent selfishness. God said: "This Qur'an guides the way to the better one" (17:9), meaning it guides the way to the higher superior self. To the same effect is His statement: "He who is guided, is guided to himself, and he who is misguided, loses his way to himself." (17:15)

As long as we remain at the level of ignorant selfishness, our freedom has to be curtailed for the benefit of society and for our own benefit as

5. The words are *dunya* (inferior) and *ukhra* (other). The same words also mean "this life," and "the next life," respectively, which is significant.

well. Such curtailment must be by means of laws which are consistent with the constitution.[6]

Thus it is clear that freedom in Islam is of two levels: the level of freedom limited by laws consistent with the constitution, as explained above, and the level of absolute freedom. A free person at the first level is one who thinks as he wishes, speaks in accordance with his thinking, and acts in accordance with his speech, on condition that his exercise of freedom of speech, or action, does not interfere with the freedom of others. If he so interferes, then his freedom is justly limited by laws which are consistent with the constitution.

A free person at the second level is one who thinks as he wishes, speaks what he thinks, and acts in accordance with what he says, and yet the consequence of his exercise of all these freedoms is only goodness, blessings, and kindness to all people. The lowest degree of the first level of freedom is fairness, while the lowest degree of the second level is forgiveness. A free man at this second level holds no ill will, even in his hidden conscience, as he knows that any such ill-will begins at the level of conscience, before it will be projected into the realm of speech, and then finally action. It is to this group that God refers in the verse: "And desist from sin, whether it is apparent or latent. Those who commit sin shall be punished with what they have committed." (6:120) He also meant these when he said: "And say that my Lord prohibited indecencies, whether apparent or latent." (7:33) Again the reference is to these when God said: "Whether you disclose what is within yourselves or keep it hidden, God will call you to account for it." (2:284)

On the other hand, the Prophet refers to people who are at the level of limited freedom when he said: "God permits for my nation what they are internally tempted to do, until they speak or act accordingly."

The two levels of freedom overlap, as the first is a preparatory stage for the second. The individual reaches the second level through his own endeavors to observe himself, hold himself to account, and morally educate himself, constantly disciplining himself towards perfection and doing good. Self-observation means awareness of the constant presence of God, so that all the senses refrain from acting in a way that displeases God, whether in thought, speech or action. Holding one's self to account means a more profound attention, in case some ill will has escaped observation. Absolute individual freedom, we have said, must be earned

6. Reference here is to the Islamic constitution, which is characterized by the reconciliation of the need of the individual to achieve absolute individual freedom with the need of the community to maintain total social justice, as explained above.

by paying its price which is, as stated above, discretion in the exercise of the freedom of the conscience, as well as freedom of speech and action. Islam has developed its worship practices and its laws in order to take the individual to that destination.

SHARI‘A IN THE SERVICE OF ABSOLUTE INDIVIDUAL FREEDOM

All the laws regulating worship and guidance practices (al-‘ibadat) are Shari‘a for the particular individual (Shari‘a fardiyah), because they concern the hidden conscience. This is so although some worship practices are performed in groups. In fact, all activities in Islam, whether in ‘ibadat, worship, or mu‘amalat, social transactions, essentially emphasize the individual conscience. Hence, the Hadith of the Prophet: "The intention of a person is better than his action."

The relationship of intention to action is similar to that of the spirit to the body: when the spirit leaves the body, the body disintegrates, decomposes and becomes scattered dust. This is subtly referred to in God's verse: "And We came to the work they have done and rendered it scattered motes." (25:23) This means that because the work was done without spirit, in other words, without being prompted by good intentions for the sake of God, it was rendered useless.

Sin begins in thought, which is the intimation of the conscience. So, if the conscience holds sin, then its thoughts shall be evil, and it will not be long before such evil thoughts prevail on the person, causing his tongue to utter them, thereby becoming manifested in evil speech. Moreover, it will not be long before this evil speech moves the speaker to a degree that is manifested in action, thereby making his actions evil too. If the individual thinks evil thoughts in his hidden conscience, speaks evil and his limbs move to do evil, then his freedom must be withdrawn and forfeited. But such forfeiture must be in the individual's own interest in the first place, and for the benefit of the community in the second place. It would be in the individual's interest to receive the education and discipline that qualify him to redeem his freedom once more, and also enable him to exercise such freedom properly.

Legislation, whether social legislation or the rules of worship, is really a disciplinary or educational method to raise communities and individuals from crudeness and hostility to refinement and humanity. The cruder and less sensitive the people, the harsher will their law be, and the more will they be limited and constrained. Thus, if people comply with their duties properly, they would suffer no hardship in either this life or the next life. God says: "God has no need for your suffering if you are thankful and believing, God is All-Thankful and All-Knowledgeable." (4:147) It is people's need for education, socialization, and discipline which brought about the prohibitions as tests of their willpower. Both prohibitions and willpower are thus completely determined by the need for them.

We have spoken at length on the need for strict limitations on individuals in early societies. When we come to modern times, the times of the monotheistic religions which we know today, we find the same exigencies without fail. The Qur'an says about the Jews:

> It is because of the transgression of the Jews that We prohibited for them things that we had previously allowed, and also because they frequently rejected the path of God and because they accepted usury although they were prohibited from taking it, and their unjustified taking of other people's property, that we have prepared for the disbelievers amongst them painful punishment. (4:160)

The Qur'an also says about the Jews:

> When Moses said to his people: Oh, my people, you have wronged yourselves by taking the calf as a god, repent to your Creator and kill yourselves as that is better for you with your Creator, may He forgive you. He is the All-Forgiving, All-Merciful. (2:54).

Thus it was because of their crudeness and insensitivity that this people suffered and had good things prohibited to them. They were subjected to the actual killing of themselves in repentance, an illustration of the principle mentioned above, namely, the use of human sacrifice as part of religious ritual in early human life on earth.

As the human individual somewhat developed, he had less need for such strictness in teaching methods. Hence the Shari'a rule for Mohamed's nation provides:

> Tell them that according to what has been revealed to me, I find that no food is prohibited except blood, and flesh of swine as it is filthy, and what has been slaughtered as an offering to one other than God, but [God forgives] whoso is driven by necessity, being neither disobedient nor exceeding the limit, surely, your Lord is Most Forgiving, Merciful. (6:145)

The Qur'an also says with respect to the nation of Mohamed: "Oh, believers, do not take each other's property by unlawful means, except what [you earn] by trade with mutual consent, and do not kill yourselves, surely God is merciful towards you." (4:29).

Thus, the circle of prohibition was reduced in the subsequent legislation, being restricted to only four items, all of which are evil. But even in relation to the four, it is permitted in cases of genuine necessity, so long as an individual is not willfully disobedient or transgressing proper limits.

God prohibited the killing of the self, when the self became responsive to a lesser degree of violence, so He said: "Do not kill yourselves, surely God is merciful towards you." He is merciful upon us in His Shari'a law, because we have also become merciful: "You shall be judged in the same you judge others."

As people became more refined, the prohibitions and limitations became more lenient, until prohibition is finally lifted from material things altogether and extended to symbolic aspects of behavior. Listen to the Qur'an:

Oh, children of Adam, put on your adornment at every time and place of worship, and eat and drink, but do not be excessive, because God does not love those who are excessive. Say: Who has forbidden adornments and good provision that God has produced for His servants? Say: They are for the believers in the present life and [will be] exclusively [for them] on the Day of Resurrection. Thus do We explain the signs for a people who have knowledge. And say that my Lord prohibited indecencies, whether apparent or latent, and unlawful transgression, and that you associate with God that for which he has sent down no authority, and that you say of God what you do not know. (7:31–33)

The Qur'an also says:

Why should you not eat of that over which the name of God has been pronounced, when He has already explained to you that which He has forbidden unto you,—save that which you are forced to do. And surely many mislead themselves by their evil desires through lack of knowledge. Assuredly, thy Lord knows best the transgressors. And desist from sin, whether it is apparent or latent. Those who commit sin shall be punished with what they have committed. (6:119–20)

Thus, what is really prohibited in the final analysis are behavioral faults and moral deficiencies. Prohibition of material things is only a means of curing the self from behavioral faults and moral deficiencies, in accordance with the rule reflected in the verse: "We shall show them Our signs in the material world, and within themselves, until it becomes manifest to them that He is the Truth. . . . Is your Lord not sufficient witness upon everything?" (41:53)

In this way prohibitions proceed from the lower material forms to subtler types of moral behavior, and then to the secrets of conscience and the thoughts of sin it entertains therein. When he said "eschew open sins as well as secret ones," the order to eschew open sins is the means to the end of eschewing secret sin. It is as if he said eschew open sin so that you may be able to eschew secret sin, which is the source of all evil. The Qur'an continues the pursuit of sin into the depths of conscience when it says: "Whether you disclose what is within yourselves or keep it hidden, God will call you to account for it." (2:284) And also when it says: "All shall submit to the Living and All-Sustaining God. And he indeed has failed who holds iniquity." (20:111) Iniquity here is subtle polytheism, which is the source of evil of every type and description. Such subtle polytheism is held in the hidden conscience, and an even subtler type of polytheism is held in what the *sufi* (Muslim mystics) call *sir al-sir* (secret of the conscience). The Qur'an refers to this: "Whether or not you speak aloud, He knows not only what is secret (*sir*) but also what is even more subtle and hidden than that." (20:7) What is even more subtle and hidden than conscience (*sir*) is the secret of the conscience (*sir al-sir*).

The Qur'an's approach to ridding the self of sin proceeds from the outside to the inside. "We shall show them Our signs in the material world, and within themselves, until it becomes manifest to them that He is the Truth. Is your Lord not a sufficient witness upon everything?" (41:53) The phrase, "We shall show them Our signs in the material world, and within themselves" generally means that the diligent worshiper along the path of God begins with observing himself, and holding himself to account for the most obvious faults of action, while permitting himself to continue in faults of speech, in accordance with a gradual process of purification. Once an individual consistently curbs his faults of action, he proceeds to the task of restraining faults of speech, while tolerating, at the same time, faults of thoughts. An individual's thoughts may remain confused and impure, as he proceeds along the path of purification.

When an individual has learned to control his body and tongue, he can begin to quiet his mind and master his thoughts. The individual thus reaches a purified state through what we call the reversed, or inverted approach, starting from the outside and proceeding ever more profoundly inward.

At this point the second portion of the above quoted verse becomes relevant: "Is your Lord not sufficient witness upon everything?" The individual is henceforth concerned primarily with his inner self, after having previously been occupied and obsessed with the outside world. This is also the point where harmony of conscience and conduct is achieved, as the purity of the conscience is manifested in the righteousness of behavior. An individual at this stage is at the threshold of absolute individual freedom. The purer the conscience the more righteous the behavior, and this in turn leads to the narrowing of the circle of prohibitions and the broadening of the circle of permissions, in accordance with the verse: "God has no need for your suffering if you are thankful and believing, God is All Thankful and All Knowledgeable." (4:147)

If the diligent worshiper advances to the desired end, namely total purity of conscience and complete righteousness of behavior, material prohibitions and restrictions disappear and the verse that applies then is: "Believers who do good deeds commit no offense whatever they eat provided they are pious and believe and do good deeds, become more pious and believe further, and again become more pious, and perfect their conduct. God loves the perfectionists." (5:93)

This is an advanced stage of absolute individual freedom, and all Islamic legislation is conceived to enable individuals to attain it. Thus, we find that all aspects of Islamic legislation are based on the principles of reciprocity (al-mu'awadah) or retribution (al-qasas). "And there is life for you [in the law of] retribution, O men of understanding, so that you become pious." (2:179) The Qur'an also says: "It is not according to your wishes nor the wishes of the People of the Book. Whoso does evil shall be penalized by it, and he shall find no refuge or supporter except God." (4:123) The Qur'an also says: "God shall reward the truthful ones by their truthfulness, and punish the hypocrites, if he wishes, or forgive them. God is All-Forgiving and All-Merciful." (33:24) Again, "Then whoso does an atom's weight of good will see it, and whoso does an atom's weight of evil will also see it." (99:7–8)

These two last verses are the essence and foundation of both the Shari'a and the truth (haqiqah), that is to say, of punishment or reward in this life as well as the next life.

The Qur'an also tells us: "That [God] may question the truthful about their truthfulness. And for the infidels He has prepared a painful punishment." [33:8] When the leader of the Sufi sect, Abu al-Qasim al-Jinayd, was asked concerning this verse, he said: "The ones who are truthful with themselves shall be asked of their truthfulness with God." God's truthfulness is absolute, while with humans it is only relative. Thus, every truthful person shall be rewarded to the extent of his truthfulness as measured against the absolute truthfulness, according to the Qur'an: "God shall reward the truthful ones by their truthfulness." This reward is retribution (qasas) in Shari'a and retribution (qasas) in the truth (haqiqah) as well, as indicated in the verse "And there is life for you [in the law of] retribution, Oh men of understanding, so that you become pious." Life in this context means additional knowledge. That is to say, when you are rewarded by goodness for the good you have done, in accordance with the rule that a good deed receives ten times as much good in reward, or even multiplied, and when you are punished for doing bad to the same degree as the bad you did, if not forgiven,[7] you shall thereby increase in life through the consequent enhancement of your comprehension, clarity of your minds, and wholesomeness of your hearts.

Such enhancement of awareness as a result of retribution in Shari'a is obvious, because an individual would not trespass on the liberties of others in the exercise of his own liberty except because of ignorance or the lack of intelligence or sensitivity. Thus, anyone who pulls out the eye of another person, in a fit of anger, for example, does not do so while fully realizing the degree of pain and the magnitude of the injury he is thereby inflicting upon his victim. If he received retribution by being placed in the same position as his victims, and his eye is pulled out in reciprocity (mu'awadah) for what he had done, then two purposes would have been served at the same time. Firstly, the interest of the community would be preserved by deterring the aggressor himself, as well as deterring others by his example. Secondly, the aggressor deepens his sensitivity, by himself experiencing the pain he inflicts upon others, and thus realizes the severity of the pain and the magnitude of the loss he has caused. There is no doubt that such a painful experience would make whoever is exposed to it more humane in his subsequent life, as he would not continue to disregard the consequences of his actions upon others. In the future, such an individual would at least abstain from hurting others and would

7.   The author is referring here to the Qur'anic rules of divine reckoning, explained on pages 101 and 103.

certainly be more considerate of others in his actions. When assisted by worship, the individual enlightened in this way would wish to do good to others, and find self-satisfaction and tranquility in doing so. Should he achieve this, he would be at the threshold of his own absolute individual freedom, as a result of a higher degree of awareness, and deeper sensitivity he received through retribution.

If an individual does not reach that point, it is enough that he at least be aware of the limits of his liberty with respect to the liberties of others, because a lot of good would come about as a result of such awareness.

Reciprocity (al-mu-'awadah) in the case of fornication is a fixed punishment (hadd) of either stoning to death or whipping.[8] Since the fornicator sought easy pleasure without regard for Shari'a, he is made to suffer pain in order to recover his senses. An individual tends to lean more towards pleasure than towards pain. By pulling the self to pain, when it succumbs to prohibited pleasure, he reestablishes a certain equilibrium and avoids recklessness and folly.

The fixed punishment for drinking alcohol is based on the same principle. A person who takes alcohol wishes to numb his mind, thereby trying to escape reality. The pain of whipping is intended to bring him back to face bitter reality, so that he may use his clear mind to improve this reality. Realities are not changed by escaping them, but rather by facing them and applying one's intellect to them. God says: "God does not change the state of any people until they change the state of themselves." (13:11)

Moreover, the mind, which is the only cause of man's superiority over animals, is the product of the interaction between pleasure and pain which accompanied life, throughout its long journey since ancient times. If an individual tries to abandon his mind in a moment of weakness, then the shock of pain will help the mind regain its control and guide its owner through the turbulence of life towards the goal of perfection.

The laws of reciprocity (al-mu'awadah) and retribution (al-qasas)—emanate from the fundamental original source of life.[9] These are not

8. A married offender is to be stoned to death while an unmarried one is given one hundred lashes. The Qur'an, however, sets such a high standard of proof, the testimony of four reliable witnesses to the actual act of intercourse (Qur'an 24:4) that it is almost impossible to prove the offense without the voluntary confession of the offender which is maintained up to and during the execution of the sentence. False accusation of fornication, which is any accusation that is unsupported by four reliable witnesses, is punishable by the hadd of eighty lashes.

9. Al-mu'awadah and al-qasas, reciprocity and retribution, respectively, are used by the author interchangeably as two levels of the same thing or two sides of the same coin, as explained below.

religious law in the common sense of the term. When we assert that the laws of Islam are based on the principle of retribution, we are referring to the essence and not the faith of Islam. Islam, in its essence, is not a religion according to the common meaning of the word, but rather a science, its dogma being merely transitional to its scientific stage. The stage of Shari'a law is also a transitional stage to the level of the truth (*haqiqah*) where individuals elevate themselves from the law of the community to the law of the individual, *Shari'a fardiyah*, which is the beginning of the truth (*haqiqah*) of each particular person.[10]

The Qur'an says: "There has, certainly, been a time when man was not a thing worth mentioning. We have created man of clear water mixed with mud and continued to test him until We made him able to hear and see." (76:1–2) This means that there has been a time when "man," meaning mankind, was not "worth mentioning," that is to say, he was passing through lower stages of development in life, before the emergence of his mind developed to the point of becoming the basis of responsibility, thereby making man a thing which is "worth mentioning." Thus, out of the "clear water mixed with mud" emerged life in the darkness of time. The phrase "continued to test him" is the essence of the whole verse as it refers to man's struggle with his natural environment and with fellow creatures. We have already discussed above some aspects of the development of human society. The struggles preceding and following the emergence of human society have been, and continue to be, conducted in accordance with the law of reciprocity (*al-mu'awadah*) and retribution (*al-qasas*).

The phrase "until We made him able to hear and see" refers to the mind, indicating that the mind is born out of the struggle, in accordance with the law of reciprocity (*al-mu'awadah*): "Then whoso does an atom's weight of good will see it. And whoso does an atom's weight of evil will also see it." (99:7–8).

Following the above quoted first two verses of *Surat al-Dahr* (chapter 76 of the Qur'an) we find the verse: "We have guided his path onto either being thankful or ungrateful." "Thankful" in this context means "right," while "ungrateful" means "wrong." In this way the mind fluctuates on the pendulum of right and wrong, which is the basis of its perfection. As the Prophet said: "If you do not make mistakes and then repent, God shall

---

10. The law of the individual (*Shari'a fardiyah*) is not inconsistant with that of the community. It is more refined and restrictive for the individual who seeks to be bound by it as a methodology for achieving absolute individual freedom over and above what is required of everybody else.

replace you with other people, who make mistakes and then repent, whence they are forgiven."

The law of reciprocity (al-mu'awadah) is of two levels: the level of the truth (haqiqah) and the level of the law (Shari'a) with a difference between the two levels in degree only and not in essence. The law of al-mu'awada at the level of the haqiqah is based on the verse, "Then whoso does an atom's weight of good will see it. And whoso does an atom's weight of evil will also see it." (99:7–8), while the law of al-mu'awadah at the level of Shari'a is based on the verse, "We have decreed in it [revelation] that a life for a life, an eye for an eye, a nose for a nose, an ear for an ear, a tooth for a tooth, and wounds are to be judged according to retribution (qasas) and he who condones, it shall be taken to his advantage, but they who do not apply what God has revealed are the unfair ones." (5:45)

The law of reciprocity (al-mu'awadah) at the level of the truth (haqiqah) is the Will with which God has molded the worlds and created them into existence and manipulated them to perfection. It is also al-haq[11] often mentioned in the Qur'an: "We have not created the heavens and the earth and what is in between except by al-haq, and for a predetermined period and yet the infidels fail to heed the warning they have been given" (46:3); "He created the heavens and the earth by al-haq. Let Him be praised and elevated above their [false] idols" (16.3); "We have not created the heavens and the earth and what is between them playfully. We have not created them except by al-haq, but most of them do not know" (44:38–39). Al-haq is this principle of retribution (al-qasas), which is reflected with perfect precision in the verse: "Then whoso does an atom's weight of good will see it. And whoso does an atom's weight of evil will also see it." (99:7–8)

The word "playfully" in the preceding verse refers to the same meaning as two other verses: "Did you think that We have created you in vain, and that you would not be brought back to Us. Exalted be God, the true King, there is no god but He, the Lord of the Glorious Throne." (23:115–16) This means that the worlds must return to God in accordance with this law of reciprocity (al-mu'awadah). "It is not according to your wishes nor the wishes of the People of the Book. Whoso does evil shall be

11. Al-haq is the opposite of al-batil (falsehood), hence it is a degree of Al-haqiqa. Al-haq is relative while al-haqiqah is absolute and ultimate truth. Al-haq is said to be the first descent of the absolute truth into the realm of duality that may be appreciated by the human mind, which can only understand anything by constrasting it to another, its opposite.

penalized by it, and he shall find no refuge or supporter except God."
(4:123)

The law of reciprocity (al-mu'awadah) at the level of the law (Shari'a)
is an accurate imitation of the law of reciprocity (al-mu'awadah) at the
level of the truth (haqiqah) and purports to follow it closely. But in its
superior manifestations, the latter (haqiqah) is infinitely subtler and more
accurate than the former (Shari'a). The law of mu'awadah at the haqiqah
level falls on three planes, as described by the verse: "God enjoins al-'adl,
justice, al-ihsan, the doing of good to others, and benevolence to the next
of kin." (16:90) "Justice" is al-qases at the level of "an eye for an eye, a
tooth for a tooth" and "Anyone who assaults you, then you may assault
him in the same way," while al-ihsan is forgiving the aggressor: "[A]nd he
who condones, it shall be taken to his advantage," as mentioned in the
verse of al-qasas. "Benevolence to the next of kin" means next of the
wider kin, that of life as a whole. These three levels are stated in the
verse: "The penalty for evil is an equal evil, but he who forgives and
reforms, his reward is upon God, He does not love the unfair ones."
(42:40) The phrase "penalty for evil is an equal evil" is the level of justice
at the degree of retribution, but God described it as "evil" in order to
discourage resort to retribution, whenever possible: "For those who are
patient and forgiving that is the best of things." (42:43) As to the phrase
"he who condones," this is the level of al-ihsan by leaving the wrongdoer
unpunished, which is superior to justice. The words "and reforms" mean
compassion with the aggressor, and kindness and tenderness with him,
and love for him, and this is the ultimate in reform and rehabilitation, and
it is the highest degree of the law of reciprocity (al-mu'awadah) in Shari'a.

The law of al-mu'awadah at the level of the haqiqah is designed to
direct the worlds to God by way of the body through molding and
compulsion. In contrast, the law of al-mu'awadah at the level of Shari'a is
designed to direct human beings through their minds and freedom,
thereby conferring full dignity on man. At this point it is appropriate to
discuss the relationship between man and the universe.

THE INDIVIDUAL AND THE UNIVERSE IN ISLAM

Man's place in the universe has been a theme of discourse and
learning since the dawn of human life until the present day. In trying to
discover the true nature of his relationship to the universe, man from the
very beginning enlisted the help of religion and science. Religion and

science have thus proceeded hand in hand since their simultaneous beginnings and throughout history.

Early man's scope of scientific knowledge was extremely limited, which increased his capacity for religious belief. He worshiped all physical phenomena within his natural environment, as well as those mysterious elements which existed beyond the physical world, revealed to him by his dreams and fantasies. His realm of scientific knowledge was limited to the few things with which he was familiar through long experience.

Early man sensed that everything in the universe had a spirit, and his dreams confirmed this feeling. So he began to pray for everything, for hunting, planting, harvesting, eating, and for weapons. But gradually familiarity and experience diminished the fear and reverence attached to things which, in time, man learned to control. Consequently, as the ambit of man's physical knowledge increased, that of his religious belief decreased. That process has culminated, today, in the assertion by some of the most extreme enthusiasts of modern science that there is no longer any place for religion in the life of civilized man. The source of this heresy, however, is not science, but some misguided scientists who have failed to appreciate the proper role of both science and religion.

Science has never claimed to deal with the essence of things, but merely their manifestations and the laws regulating their behavior. Science knows the qualities of electricity, but not its essence. Moreover, science itself acknowledges that matter, as we know it, is merely the manifestation of something beyond, unknown to us. Einstein stated that matter and energy are one and the same thing, and experiments splitting the atom confirmed the truth of that statement. The essence of energy is unknown, though some of the laws regulating its conduct are known.

In fact, modern science is the most eloquent and persuasive pro-pagandist for God. It is continuously showing us that if we study the material world, it will indicate a supernatural world beyond it—a world which is inconceivable to our senses in the normal manner. Science leaves us standing alone, in awe and reverence, and seeking methods other than those of science to guide us into the mysteries of the holy valley that lies beyond the material world which we know.

People with developed awareness hear material phenomena call to God in a loud voice that says: We are temptation and trial, do not become infidels! Your objective is ahead, do not stay with us.

It is time for man to appreciate that the environment in which he lives is a spiritual environment with material manifestations. This con-clusion, proved through recent developments in modern science, faces

man with a clear challenge—to reconcile himself with both environ-
ments as a condition for survival.

Early man was wiser than we are now, since he believed, or rather
appreciated, that everything in the universe has a spirit. History repeats
itself in cycles, and a new cycle is imminent. As indicated earlier, this will
not occur in exactly the same way, but rather in a manner that is similar in
some respects, though different in others, from previous experience. We
shall again become aware of the fact that our environment is spiritual in
essence, though material in manifestation. The difference, on the other
hand, shall be in that such awareness, this time, shall not be naive and
ignorant, but rather intelligent and knowledgeable, so that religion will
be the guide to all our activities. Religion will again become important,
but this time with a universal and scientific approach to life. It shall
respectfully address the mind, and seek to convince it of the utility of
adopting a religious approach to everyday life, both with respect to
subsistence in this life as well as for the purposes of the next life.

Man has no design or option in coming into this life, and he shall
have none on leaving it. Of this God tells us:

> We have created man of an extraction of clay. Then We set him, a drop,
> in a secure receptacle. Then We created the drop into a clot, then We
> created of the clot a tissue, then We created of the tissue bones, and
> covered the bones with flesh, then We transformed him into a different
> being. So blessed be God, the best of creators. Then after you shall all
> surely die. And on the Day of Resurrection you shall surely be raised.
> (23:12–16)

This comprehensive Qur'anic image illustrates our position in the universe, where we are manipulated in the same way dead matter is manipulated. We shall not be superior to such dead matter unless we fully
appreciate this fact, and surrender to it willingly and knowingly.

God has endowed us with the potential to acquire this knowledge. He
referred to this potential in the above mentioned verse by the phrase
"then We transformed him into a different being." In another place the
meaning is very clear, where God said: "When your Lord told the angels I
am making a human being out of dry ringing clay of black mud wrought
into shape. So, when I have fashioned him, and breathed into him from
My Spirit, you shall submit to him" (15:28–29). Thus, this different being
came about as a result of the breathing of God's Spirit into him.

THE WILL

God's spirit which was breathed into man is the will. The will is an intermediate attribute falling beneath knowledge but above ability. God brought the universe into being through knowledge, will, and ability. Human beings also act through knowledge, will, and ability. Thus, the creature is modeled after the Creator. This is what the Prophet meant when he said: "God has created Adam after His own image."

The true will is that of God, while man has will only on loan. This loan is the trust referred to in the verse: "We have offered the trust to the heavens and earth and the mountains, but they refused to take it, and were fearful of it. Man accepted it; he is surely unfair and ignorant." (33:72) Man is "unfair" in claiming for himself what belongs to another, and he is "ignorant" of his own worth when he believes that he has [an independent] will. But he was deluded into this unfairness and ignorance by the subtlety of the whole affair. God be praised in His Wisdom, manipulated various gasses, liquids, and dead matter in a direct and compelling manner:

> Say, you are disbelieving in Him who created the earth in two days, and do you set compeers to Him? He is the Lord of all being, and made upon it [the earth] mountains and blessed it, and ordained therein its suste-nance in four days, equal for those who ask. Then He came upon the heaven, which was in smoke, and He told it and the earth, come in obedience or compulsion, and they replied, We come in obedience, and He ordained them seven heavens in two days, and revealed to each heaven its order, and We decorated the lower heaven with lambs and security, that is the ordainment of the All-Powerful, All-Knowledge-able. (41:9)

This is the environment of life. So when the scene was set on earth, God created life and endowed it with "the will to live," a force that is motivated by self-preservation, the pursuit of pleasure, and avoidance of pain. In that way God manipulated creatures at the level of plants and animals, in a semi-direct way, behind the veil of "the will to live." The term "the will to live" means that life, at that stage, enjoyed spontaneous movement appearing to have inherent motivation and power of move-ment. The living organism utilized its power to move and collect its food and preserve its life and its species.

When God promoted life to the level of a human being, he added to "the will to live" a new factor, namely, "the will to be free," which differs from the will to live in degree only rather than in essence. God thus manipulated man through the will to live, and then through the will to be free, and thereby He began to manipulate us indirectly, and to be present in our affairs in such a subtle and fine way that we were deluded with the belief that we possess an independent will to act. In this context we may refer to some verses which clearly illustrate the subtlety of the intervention of God's Will in directing our will:

> When you were on the near bank [of the valley] and they were on the farther bank, and the cavalcade was below you, and if you were to make an appointment, you would have surely failed to meet. [But the meeting was arranged for you] so that God might determine a matter that was done, so that those who perish, do so on a clear position, and those who live, do so also on a clear position, God is All-Hearing, All-Knowledgeable. When God showed them to you in your dream as few, and if He had shown them to you as many, you would certainly have faltered and would have disagreed with one another about the matter; but God saved [you]. Surely, He has full knowledge of what is in [your] hearts. At the time of your encounter, He made them appear to you as few in your eyes, and made you [appear] as few in their eyes, so that God might determine a matter that was done: and unto God all things shall return. (8:42–44)

Look at this amazing subtlety as the eternal divine will intervenes to manipulate the transient human will!

The Prophet in his sleep sees his enemy as few, and therefore resolves to fight them; and if he saw them differently he would not have resolved to fight. At the moment of encounter, the believers see the nonbelievers as few, so they resolve to fight them; and the nonbelievers see the believers as few, and so they also resolve to fight them. It is God who shows each party their enemy as few, in order to bring about a predetermined event.[12] All that is achieved without disturbing "the will to be free" or making it feel any outside interference in its affairs, or any dictation or abrogation of its freedom.

God created man weak and without claws or sharp teeth so that he should rely on his wit rather than his physical strength. He also made

12. These verses of the Qur'an relate the events of the battle of *Badr*, the first decisive battle that the Muslims won, thereby ensuring the survival of their infant community of believers in Medina.

man's childhood long so that he should depend on others rather than be independent. Thus, his weakness and long childhood compelled him to live in groups. We have already discussed the beginnings of communities and how they established customs and inhibited the impulses of individuals. Death was the penalty imposed upon any individual who violated the custom approved by the community. Moreover, the anger of the gods could also await the individual after his death, to torture him further. Thus, the fear of the community's anger, and that of the gods, haunted individuals and still prompts them to refrain from violating the law.

With the establishment of primitive human society, two forces within the human being came into conflict; the ancient animal motivated by "the will to live" and its preoccupation with the pursuit of pleasure, and the newborn human being motivated by "the will to be free." While the latter force was directed towards the pursuit of pleasure, it was subject to the condition that the individual did not displease the community or the gods by violating accepted customs. Violation would bring as its consequence lasting pain in this life and also after death.

If the desired pleasure could not be attained without violating the directives of the community, which were always those of the gods, "the will to be free" would abandon the pursuit of that pleasure, in the hope of attaining the greater pleasure or reward of the community and that of the gods, a better and longer lasting reward. In that way, values were introduced whereby the individual sacrificed immediate pleasure, or sacrificed immediate material pleasure, in expectation of immediate or delayed spiritual rewards, such as the approval, confidence, and praise of the society, or the approval of the gods and their reward, whether in this life or in the next.

Human society continued to develop, while its customs and traditions became more established and refined. The prophets came, and with them the concept of right and wrong, permissible and impermissible, ideas of heaven and hell and the qualities of God. The prophets and messengers to humanity did not come to tell the people that they have a Creator, as that was already established by the messengers of the intellect.[13] They [the prophets] came to help mankind appreciate the Creator by teaching His attributes, qualities, and deeds.

The distinguishing powers of the mind evolved from the continuing interaction between "the will to live" and "the will to be free." Gradually,

---

13. These are men of superior intellect who reached this rational conclusion without receiving heavenly revelation.

the mind escaped from ancient fears which were cast into the heart of early man by the presence of uncontrollable forces within his natural environment.

As stated above, the will to be free differs from the will to live only in degree and not in essence. In other words, the will to be free is the more refined and subtle side of the will to live. Hence, the will to be free is the spirit, while the will to live is the self. The will to live is the female of the human beings, while the will to be free is the male, the mind being the offspring of the interaction of the two.[14] At the level of this interaction which produces the mind, the will to live is called the memory, while the will to be free is the imagination. Memory is the outcome of all previous experiences, hence we called it the self in another context.

We stated earlier that retribution (al-qasas) is designed to reinforce the power of sensitivity upon anyone who needs to experience what he had inflicted upon his victim. Sensitivity is really another name of intelligence, which is the power of comprehension and control or repression of those selfish desires which contravene the law. In regulating selfish desires, intelligence is motivated by fear—in other words, through the action of desire or fear upon the mind. The strength and discriminatory power of the intelligence increases with its ability to control the selfish desires. On the other hand, the self becomes more and more obedient, or mutinous, depending on whether the intelligence is fair and considerate, or extremist and violent in its handling of those selfish desires.

The mind had an unhappy childhood because it was born in a divided home, with two quarrelsome parents—a lustful and rebellious mother, and a weak and cowardly father who tended to be harsh and violent to the extent of being unnecessarily repressive. In fact, the mind had a delinquent, truant, and bitter childhood, reflecting the characteristics of its parents and the effects of the home in which it was born. Hence, the mind, too, became divided and labored under inner conflict. As the saying goes: "A divided home shall not stand."

Fear has manifested itself in the lowest depths of the self since the beginning of life, even before man came onto the scene.[15] Then followed

14. The author is using here analogies and metaphors from the literature and traditions of the Sufi (Islamic mystics) with whom he has a strong affinity and common cultural ground.

15. The author maintains that man evolved from earlier beings—as briefly explained below. His religious evolutionary theory is discussed in detail, and substantiated by religious texts and arguments, in the Introduction to the fifth edition of his book Risalat al-Salah (A Treatise on Prayer) (in Arabic).

the long conflict between "the will to live" and "the will to be free" which accompanied the coming of man and has continued to the present day. As a result of this conflict, some objectionable desires, which previously had free expression, were inhibited and curtailed, and thus incarcerated in the dark dungeons of the fringes of the self. All these desires are original, and many of them were locked up in the dark for so long that they lost their sight and ability to move, but they are by no means dead. They merely await the day of their liberation.

The human self is beset with much pestilence. There is the fear it acquired since the dawn of its primitive life, before it even became human. Then man came onto the scene, to inherit inhibitions which had accumulated since the beginning of human society up to the time an individual is born. There is also the inhibition acquired during one's own individual lifetime, from his birth to his death, because the law, custom, and public opinion continue to operate in inhibiting objectionable desires and denying them both expression and freedom of action.

Fear is the cause of all inhibition. In that way, fear, whether primitive, naive, and unfounded, or intelligent, balanced, and well-founded, has left its permanent imprint on the human self.

Fear, whatever form it takes, is the legitimate father of all moral perversion and behavioral distortion. Man will never perfect his manhood, and woman will never perfect her womanhood, as long as they remain frightened to any degree or in any fashion. Perfection is obtained through the process of liberation from fear.

The individual will never be liberated from all forms of inherited fear except through complete knowledge of the environment in which he lived, and continues to live, and which was the direct cause of the precipitation of fear into the lowest depth of his being. Fear is ignorance, and ignorance can be eliminated only by knowledge. That is why it is imperative that the individual be given a full and true picture of his relationship with society and with the universe at large. This has been our concern for some time now.

DETERMINISM AND FREE WILL (AL-JABR WA AL-IKHTIYAR)

The question of determinism and free will represents the essence of the relationship between the individual and the universe. It is a problem that in its finer points has troubled human thought in all ages. It is time for the problem to command our attention once more, because the need for its full understanding is not an idle, intellectual luxury or a problem that is irrelevant to our daily life. The importance of understanding this problem is due to the need for the scientific approach to be utilized in the attainment of absolute individual freedom. Absolute individual freedom is, as of today, the center from which social freedom, in all its forms and levels, branches out and radiates.

The ongoing question is whether man is manipulated to a predetermined destiny (*musayr*) or enjoys genuine choice (*mukhayr*).

The Prophet had settled this question to the full satisfaction of the believers when he said: "Anyone who believes has done so according to predetermined judgment and fate, and anyone who disbelieves has also done so according to a predetermined judgment and fate; the pens are suspended and the pages are dry [that is, everything is already settled once and for all]." When some of his companions said: "Why all the labor, O, Messenger of God?" He replied: "Do your labor; everyone is guided to what he has been created for." The Companions of the Prophet then went about their business and held fast to their faith, which protected and comforted them. "Those who believe and do good deeds shall be guided by their faith, and they shall have rivers flowing beneath their feet in Paradise." (10:9)

The needs of a believer (*mu'min*) are satisfied by faith as such, but the needs of a *muslim* require more knowledge, which leads him to the threshold of certainty and tranquillity of the heart.[16] Take the Prophet Abraham, for example:

When Abraham said: 'Oh Lord, show me how you can bring the dead back into life.' His Lord said: 'Do you not believe?' He replied: 'Yes, I do, but I want to set my heart at ease.' [His Lord] said: 'Take four birds, cut them into pieces, put each part on a mountain, then call them and they shall come to you in haste, and then you shall know that God is All Able, and All Wise.' (2:260)

The Companions of the Prophet were followed by those who were unable to accept what the Companions accepted. It seemed to some of them, known as the rationalists, that determinism coupled with punish-

16. A *muslim* is one who enjoys genuine submission to God, as opposed to a *mu'min*, who is merely a believer in the sense explained in the introduction to the third edition of this book.

ment for sin amounts to, as the poet put it: "He threw him in water all tied up and fettered, and yet told him not to get wet."[17]

They argued that since this would obviously be unjust, and as God is totally above causing any injustice, and as punishment for sin is clearly stated in Shari'a law and in religion it follows, then, that man enjoys a degree of choice which renders him liable to punishment when he commits a mistake and entitles him to reward when he does right. This was their belief, which amounts to associating other gods with God, while they set out to achieve the opposite result.

This fallacy was supported by two factors. Firstly, common sense and appearances suggest that man has a choice as reflected in his voluntary movements. He can walk when he wants, or sit, or stand, etc., all movements falling under his control and free will. Secondly, the Qur'an apparently confirms what common sense provides.

The *sufis*, on the other hand, generally tried to accept the Companions' approach. Some *sufis* maintained that although man's fate is predetermined in every aspect of his life, that is, that man is manipulated to predetermined destiny *(musayr)*, the fact that he is held to account for his conduct does not mean that God is being unjust or unfair, because God is acting within His own dominion, as Creator of the world. Other *sufis* simply asserted both determinism and human accountability, without raising the question of the apparent injustice of this position, by quoting the Qur'anic verse: "He cannot be questioned as to what He does, but they will be so questioned." (21:23)

The most learned of the *sufis* agreed, however, that the conciliation of determinism, which necessarily follows from *tawhid* [God is the only actor and creator] and human accountability, on the one hand, and Divine Justice, on the other, is to be sought in the purpose or rationale of punishment. They explained this to an extent that was sufficient for the needs of their time, and the ages that followed up to the present day. But we do not believe it to be sufficient for the needs of modern thought.

THE QUR'AN AND DETERMINISM AND FREE WILL

The rationalists based their view on the Qur'an, and cited verses in support of their claim. The *sufis* who were totally opposed to the ra-

17. The author is referring here in brief outline to the long and well-known controversy in Islamic history between the rationalists, who maintained that a human being has full freedom of choice, and others, who maintained that the fate of every human being is fully and totally pre-determined by God in every detail of his or her life, irrespective of apparent free will.

tionalists' view also based their view on the Qur'an, and cited clear verses in support of their own claim. This curious phenomenon has led many Orientalists who have studied the Qur'an into mistakenly asserting that the Qur'an was self-contradictory, thereby misleading themselves and their compatriots. In fact, the Qur'an has an apparent meaning (*zahir*) and hidden meaning (*batin*). Its *zahir* is concerned with the appearance of things, while its *batin* is based on the truth beyond such appearances. The Qur'an adopted, as an educational approach, appearances as a bridge over which the learned cross to the inside. To this effect, the Qur'an says: "We shall show them Our signs in the material world, and within themselves, until it becomes manifest to them that He is the Truth. . . . Is your Lord not a sufficient witness upon everything?" (41:53)

Outside appearances are the signs in the material world, while the inside is the signs within the human self. The doors leading from the signs of the material world to the mind are the senses, and all the senses are in pairs, right and left, which also vary in strength. Thus, what the right eye conveys to the mind about a visible object is different from what the left eye conveys. Neither by itself is able to render the truth. This means that the mind has to sift the information in order to rid itself of what is known as deception of the senses, in order to arrive at the truth.

Many minds are unable to liberate themselves from the bondage of the senses, and all minds are very much dependent on the information provided by the senses. As the Qur'an is a book of dogma (faith) as well as Shari'a (law) and truth (*haqiqah*) and as there is no way to arrive at the truth (*haqiqah*) except through dogma and Shari'a, and as it was not in the interest of the dogma to contradict the information perceived by the eye, the Qur'an came with an appearance (*zahir*) consistent with the illusion of the material world as provided by our senses, and a hidden meaning (*batin*) based on the clear truth. The Qur'an, in keeping with our illusion, was protecting us against unnecessary hardship until it gradually transferred us to the truth.

Let us take two examples, one from the Qur'an in keeping with the superficial illusion of the senses, and the other in keeping with the subtle illusion of the mind:

First, as the Qur'an was propagating the faith to a people who saw the earth with their own eyes as a flat surface, it did not want to add to the difficulty of propagating the faith in God, the difficulty in advocating a new idea about the earth which was inconsistent with what is obviously seen by the eye. Hence, it provided verses about the earth which did not disturb its audience in their common belief about the earth. So it said: "We have built the heavens with Our Hands and We have vast powers.

And We spread out the earth in an excellent way" (51:47–48); "Have We not made the earth flat, and made the mountains as bulwarks?" (78:6–7); "And the earth, thereafter, He has spread forth. He produced therefrom water and pastures" (79:31–32); and "And the earth We have spread out, and set therein firm mountains, and caused everything to grow therein in proper proportion." (15:19)

Once Muslims embraced the faith and practiced Shari'a, they would realize that the earth was not flat, except as perceived by the naked eye. Yet, we cannot discover the truth of the matter if we either completely disregard what is perceived by the eye, or if we remain captive to the illusion of our senses. The rational approach is to make what the eyes perceive as a bridge to what the mind perceives, which is al-haq (relative truth), thereby eventually leading to the intermittent appreciation of the ultimate truth (haqiqah) by the heart.[18]

The example taken from the Qur'an, in keeping with the illusion of the mind, is told in the following two verses: "It is up to each one of you to take the straight path if each so wishes. But you cannot wish except what God, the Lord of the worlds, wishes." (81:28–29) When the diligent worshiper (al-salik), at the beginning, reads the verses, he understands from the first verse that he has an independent will which is free to go straight or to deviate, and he understands from the second verse only the meaning language gives. So he endeavors to his best ability to be on the straight path. When his experience matures by such endeavor and self-discipline, he comes to know for certain that he has no independent will, and that God has all will. Then he is faced with the second verse: "But you cannot wish, except what God, the Lord of the worlds, wishes," and he knows that the verse "It is up to each one of you to take the straight path if each so wishes" is abrogated with respect to himself after he has rid himself of the mind's illusion, while at the same time fully appreciating the reason why the abrogated verse was revealed in the first place.

Thus, the Qur'an has rendered its meanings in a duality: a meaning close to the apparent (zahir) level, and another meaning that is closer to the subtlety of the inner, hidden meaning (batin). But the rationalists failed to appreciate this, and they relied on the verses which were consistent with the illusions of the senses and the illusions of the mind, and derived their theories from these verses, thereby misleading themselves and others.

18. Note the difference of degree between al-haq and al-haqiqah indicated in note 11 and the accompanying text of this chapter.

The *sufis* appreciated this fact and knew that the illusions of the senses and illusions of the mind must both be discarded through diligent worship, so as to reach the level of certainty, covered by the veils of darkness and the veils of light.

THE QUR'AN AND DETERMINISM

"We reveal from the Qur'an what is healing and mercy on the believers, and only adds to the loss of the unfair ones." (17:82) The unfair ones include those who rely completely on the mind to understand the facts of religion.

The Qur'an concentrates in many of its verses on making minds understand determinism, so that once the comprehension by minds settles into the hearts, it becomes clear that there is not even a single letter in the Qur'an that does not advocate the Unity of the Actor (*wahdat al-fa'il*),[19] This principle of the Unity of the Actor (*wahdat al-fa'il*) is the origin and very foundation of the *tawhid*.[20] It is only after mastering *wahdat al-fa'il* that other levels of *tawhid* follow. Listen to the following verses:

It is He who conducts you on land, and at sea, so that once you are on a boat and it had a good wind, and they were pleased with it, a storm breaks out, and waves come from everywhere, and they believe that they are doomed, whence they pray to God in earnest: If You save us from this one, we shall be grateful. Once He saves them, they set about committing unjustified excesses on earth. . . . Oh, people, these excesses are against yourselves, and merely for cheap pleasure in this life, then you shall return to Us when We shall tell you everything you have done. (10:22–23).

This is the clearest statement on divine determinism. It refers to the cause of human ignorance and inadvertence, namely, human capabilities. For, when in facing our problems, we succeed, we are misled by such

19. The term literally means the unity of the actor or author, creator, etc. In religious context, it refers to the notion that God is the sole creator or perpetrator of all things in the universe, big and small. As He is the only one with original and effective will, ability and power, it follows that He is the sole actor or author of things, actions, etc.
20. Since *tawhid* is the belief in a single God as the sole Creator and Actor of all things and actions, hence the implications of Divine Control of every being and thing.

success into believing that we have effective will power. Opportunity for human endeavor on land is greater than it is at sea; that is why He said, "He guides you on land and at sea" [that is, He guides you in safety as well as in peril or danger]. The verses then proceed to spell out the dangers of the sea which demonstrate the futility of our efforts; hence, as the Qur'an put it, "whence they pray to God in earnest: If You save us from this one, we shall be grateful." As such prayer comes from their whole being, God saves them, and then He tells us what they did afterwards: "Once He saves them, they set about committing unjustified excesses on earth," meaning that once they escape the dangers of the sea and come ashore, and feel their ability to endeavor once more, they revert to their ignorance and inadvertance and claim that they have will power and freedom of choice. The Qur'an is reminding us here that He who guides us on land is the same One who guides us at sea, and we should not be unmindful of this.

Several Qur'anic verses emphasize this message. For example: "I have put my trust in God, my Lord and your Lord. There is no creature but He holds it under His control. Surely, my Lord is on the straight path." (11:56) "Do they seek other than the Religion of God, to Whom all those in heavens and earth have already surrendered, whether willingly or unwillingly, and to Whom they shall return?" (3:83)

". . . 'Or, do they assign to God partners who have created the like of His creation so that the [two] creations appear similar to them?' Say, 'God [alone] is the Creator of all things, and He is the One, the Most Supreme.'" (13:16) "The seven heavens and the earth and those that are therein extol His glory; and there is not a thing but glorifies Him with His praise, but you understand not their glorification. He is forbearing, most forgiving." (17:44) "Whereas God has created you and [also] your hand-iwork." (37:96) "There befalls no calamity either in the earth or in your own persons, but is recorded in a Book before We bring it into being. Surely, that is easy for God. Thus it is so that you may not grieve over what is lost to you nor exult because of that which He has bestowed upon you. And God loves not any conceited boaster, such as are niggardly and enjoin others to be niggardly. And whoso turns his back should know that God is self-sufficient, worthy of all praise." (57:22–24) In all these verses there is a great educational value for the benefit of those who are certain within themselves about the principle of determinism (tasir).

WHAT DOES DETERMINISM MEAN?

It must first be emphasized that God does not manipulate or guide people to sin, but rather to be and do right. God says through the Prophet

Hud: "I have put my trust in God, my Lord, and your Lord. There is no creature but He holds it under His control. Surely, my Lord is on the straight path." (11:56) This means that God is manipulating every being in order to put each on the straight path, and every creature will be saved, either immediately or ultimately, as long as it remains obedient to God, and nothing in the universe escapes this obedience. God, however, wants the obedient ones to obey intelligently and knowingly. Hence, He draws the line to distinguish between guidance and misguidance: anything below the line is misguided. At this point the concept of belief and unbelief comes into play.

The difference between belief and unbelief is not a difference in essence, but only in degree. The believer's knowledge is greater than that of the unbeliever. One may say that the believer obeys God knowingly, while the unbeliever obeys God unknowingly. God says: "God knows that they are worshiping no one but Himself, God is the Irresistible and the Wise." (29:42) He knows, but they do not know, and He wants them to know: "Say, are those who know equal to those who know not." (39:9)

The will of God is never disobeyed, but God wants to transform creatures from obeying what He wills to obeying what He approves, for He may will something which He does not approve. He says in the Qur'an: "If you are ungrateful, surely God is Self-Sufficient, and He is not pleased with ingratitude in His creation. But if you are grateful, He approves that for you." (39:7) Accordingly, He says if you disbelieve, you have not done so against His will; it is His will that you shall disbelieve, but He does not approve what He had willed for you. Approval is the fine end of the will. It is the peak of the pyramid based on the will. The will is at the stage of duality (thuna'yah), while approval is at the stage of singularity or unity (fardyah). The will accommodates both belief as well as unbelief, while approval accommodates belief alone.

The Creational Decree (al-'amr al-takwiny) is higher than the will. Its peak is "approval" while its base is "will," hence it is a complete pyramid. This is explained at the end of Surat Ya Sin [that is, chapter 36 of the Qur'an] where God says: "His command, when He intends a thing, He tells it to be, and it comes into being." (36:82) Legislative Decree (al-'amr al-tashri'y) represents the peak of the Creational Decree when the will is its base. So when the Almighty said: "When We wish to destroy a village, We decree that its affluent inhabitants commit sin, thereby the village becomes worthy of destruction, so We destroy it." (17:16) He is referring here to the Creational Decree at the level of the base of the pyramid, which is the will. When He said: "When they commit sin, they say we found our fathers doing it, and God has enjoined it upon us. Say God never enjoins sin. Do you say of God that which you know not." (7:28) He refers in the last quoted verse to the Legislative Decree. The phrase "God never enjoins sin" means that He does not send messengers, supported by miracles, with laws calling for the commission of sin:

> It does not befit a truthful man that God should give him the Book and wisdom and prophethood and then he should say to people: Worship me instead of God. But he would say: Be solely devoted to the Lord because you teach and study the Book. Nor would he bid you take the angels and the prophets for lords. What! would he enjoin you to disbelieve after you have surrendered to God? (3:79–80)

The Legislative Decree is a call to bring people from God's will to His approval. For that reason He had sent messengers, and revealed the Books in which He said: "God enjoins al-'adl, justice, al-ihsan, the doing of good to others, and benevolence to the next of kin, and forbids indecency, manifest evil, and transgression. He admonishes you so that you may take heed." (16:90)

Although the Legislative Decree is a unit, when contrasted with the will, on close examination one finds that it too is of the pyramid shape, with the general law of the community as its base, and Shari'a fardiyah, the law for the individual, as its peak. This peak of the Legislative Decree is the base in relation to the peak of the Creational Decree, which proceeds to God in infinity. It is to this extremely fine peak that God referred when He said: "We have created everything for its time (bi-qadar), and Our Decree is but a unit, like the blink of an eye." (54:49–50) In this way, the pyramid of the creatures becomes clearly apparent, its peak being the first descent to the level of the name (al-ism),[21] which is the stage of Shari'a fardiyah, the law for the individual person; and its base and final descent to the level of the action (al-fi'l),[22] which is the level of multiplicity, in living organisms and the elements, the least of which is smoke, that is, water vapor, out of which all things and beings were created. God said:

21. God reveals himself through stages: descending from infinitude to the level of the name, al-ism, which is the stage at which He may be referred to by the names He gave Himself, for example, God.

22. The level of action, al-fi'l, refers to the stage of creation and action in the levels of descent from the infinitude of the Supreme Divine Being.

Then He turned to the heaven, while it was smoke [gas] and said to it and to the earth: Come both of you [in obedience] willingly or unwillingly. They said: We come willingly. So he ordained them [in the form of] seven heavens in two days, and He revealed to each heaven its function. And We adorned the lowest heaven with lamps [for light] and [provided it with the means of] protection. That is the Decree of the Mighty, the All-Knowing. (41:11–12)

Even closer than this to the base of the pyramid of creation is what God said of "smoke": "Do the infidels not see that the heavens and earth were a closed-up [mass] then We opened them out? And We made of water every living being. Will they not then believe?" (21:30)

While the peak of the pyramid was with God, its base was removed from Him, not in distance but in degree.[23] The peak of the pyramid of creation, which is the level of *Shari'a fardiya*, the law of the individual, is in the realm of knowledge. The base of the pyramid is in the physical world. The realm of knowledge dominates the world of being, to the extent that the physical world is the world of appearance, while the realm of knowledge is the world of essence. In other words, the physical world is the world of corporeal things, where there is plurality, while the realm of knowledge is the world of incorporeal things, where there is unity. This does not mean there is no corporeal thing in the realm of knowledge, but it means that its corporeal things are so fine that they cannot be sensed except through the seventh sense. The *sufi* master Ibn al-Farid was referring to this excellence of spirituality when he said: "The refinement of form in reality follows the subtlety of the substance, and the form, in turn, enhances the substance." This means that for every meaning there is a corporeal existence, and for every truth (*haqiqah*) there is a corresponding Shari'a. Every meaning or every truth (*haqiqah*) has a pyramid shape, with a peak and a base. The finer the peak becomes, the finer the base is in consequence. In other words, the finer the meaning the finer is its corporeal existence.

God said: "Be praised He Who holds the essence of everything, and to Him you shall return." (36:83) The essence of everything is its individuality. The phrase "and to Him you shall return" emphasizes this understanding, because return to God shall be by closing the gap between the qualities of the slave and the qualities of the Lord. It is as if all

---

23. Since God is not contained in space or time, things cannot be removed from Him in distance, but rather in value or degree.

creatures are conducted to achieve their individuality in their totality, from plurality to unity by way of monotheism *(tawhid)*. God says:

> By the fig and the olive and by Mount Sinai and by this safe house, We have created man in the best mold. Then We reduced him to the bottom of creation. But those who believed and did good deeds shall have unlimited reward. What makes them disbelieve in religion? Is God not the wisest of the rulers? (95:1–8)

We have said earlier that the *zahir* or apparent meaning of the Qur'an deals with the physical environment, while its *batin* or deeper meaning deals with the spiritual features of the human self. God's concern is for the human being, and not the heavens and the earth. An ant is greater in God's esteem than the sun, because the ant has come into the chain of life and death, while the sun awaits its turn to enter this advanced stage. Here we are not dealing with the apparent or superficial *(zahir)* meaning of these verses, which may easily be obtained in any book of interpretation of the Qur'an.[24]

God swears by Himself when He swears by the forces of the human self. "Oh, people, fear your Lord Who created you from a single Self and of it [too] He created a mate, and from the twain spread many men and women; and fear God, in Whose Name you appeal to one another, and [fear Him particularly respecting] ties of kinship. Verily, God watches over you." (4:1)

This one Self out of which He created us in His Own Self, be He praised and revered. I swear by "the fig" is the self, and "olive" the spirit, and "Mount Sinai" the mind, and "this safe house" the heart. We have already mentioned that the mind is the result of the fertilization of the self by the spirit, and we say in this context that the mind is the guide of the heart and its pioneer in pursuit of knowledge. It is to the heart like the walking stick of a blind man, with which he senses his way. The relationship of the mind to the heart is like the relationship of the five senses to the mind itself. When the mind is strengthened and sharpened, and begins to receive its awareness from all the senses at every moment, it becomes the forthcoming sixth sense. Life began with a single sense, and then developed in ancient times to the second sense, then the third, the

---

24. The author seeks *ta'wyl*, which is the deeper and more insightful meaning of the Qur'an as distinguished from *tafsyr*, which is the superficial plane of meaning of the Arabic text of the Qur'an.

fourth, and the fifth. It is now proceeding on its way to the sixth and seventh senses. Further development shall be through improving these same seven senses, and not through increasing their number. The sixth sense is, then, the mind, when it sharpens and becomes able simultaneously to taste, smell, touch, see, and hear everything.

When the mind reaches this stage, it will know its own worth, and realize that its place is behind the heart and not before it [that is, to be led by the heart rather than to lead it]. It will hear, and try to obey the saying of the learned *sufi* al-Jinad: "Follow a leader whom you used to lead." Obedience to this order is, however, most difficult for the mind, and it shall not be achieved except from time to time, at the peak of self-discipline. When achieved, it is not maintained for long, as the *Khidr* of the heart tells the Moses of the mind: "You shall not be able to be patient with me."25 Nevertheless, this short moment which the Moses of each person endures with his Khidr is worth eternal time, as it is outside time. It is the level of "the eye deviated not, nor did [it] wander" (53:17), where the diligent worshiper perceives Him who is not contained in time. This is the level of witnessing the Supreme Being *(al-dhat)* through abandonment of all intermediaries, whereupon the heart becomes the seventh sense, and whereby the diligent worshiper becomes unitary.

But the mind is soon overtaken by its weakness, and it becomes ignorant of its own worth, and oversteps the heart. Hence, the diligent worshiper becomes a duality, veiled by the mind from witnessing the Supreme Being *(al-dhat)* and able to see only its manifestations at the levels of name, quality, and action, the lowest level of which is the Unity of the Actor level of *wahdat al-fa'il*. The diligent worshiper at the level of the veils of light still suffers from subtle polytheism, but he does have his *Shari'a fardiyah,* his own individual law, and as such, he is in his own realm of essence.

God's expression in the above-mentioned verses, "We have created man in the best mold," refers to man's creation in the realm of essence, which is the peak of the pyramid of creation, that being in the world of decree; while the part, "Then We reduced him to the bottom of creation" refers to man's creation in the physical world, which is the base of the pyramid of creation, that being the world of creatures: "He holds the creation as well as the decree." (7:54) The Qur'an also says: "We have

25. The metaphoric reference is to the Qur'anic story of Moses' experience with a knowledgeable holy man (the Qur'an 18:65–82), where Moses stands for pure rational thinking while *Khidr* stands for the deeper insight of the heart.

created everything for its time *(bi-qadar)*, and Our Decree is but a unit, like the blink of an eye." (54:49–50)

The story of man's creation in the best mold, and then his reduction to the bottom of creation, is told in the following verses:

> And when thy Lord said to the angels, "I am about to place a viceregent in the earth," they said, "Wilt Thou place therein such as will cause disorder in it and shed blood?—and we glorify Thee with Thy praise and extol Thy holiness." He answered, "I know what you know not." And He taught Adam all the names, then He put [the objects of] these [names] before the angels and said, "Tell Me the names of these, if you are right." They said, "Holy art Thou! No knowledge have we except what Thou hast taught us; surely, Thou art the All-Knowing, the Wise."
>
> He said, "O Adam, tell them their names;" and when he had told them their names, He said, "Did I not say to you, I know the secrets of the heavens and of the earth, and I know what you reveal and what you hide?" And [remember the time] when We said to the angels, "Submit to Adam," and they [all] submitted. But *Iblis* [did not].[26] He refused and deemed himself too big; and he was of the disbelievers. And We said, "O Adam, dwell thou and thy wife in the garden, and eat therefrom plentifully wherever you will, but approach not this tree, lest you be of the wrongdoers." But Satan caused them both to slip by means of it and drove them out of [the state] in which they were. And We said, "Go forth hence; some of you are enemies of others and for you there is an abode in the earth and a provision for a time." Then Adam learnt from his Lord certain words [of prayer]. So He turned towards him with mercy. Surely, He is Oft-Returning [with compassion, and is] Merciful. We said, "Go forth hence, all of you. And if there comes to you guidance from Me, then whoso shall follow My guidance, on them [shall come] no fear nor shall they grieve." But they who will disbelieve and treat Our Signs as lies, these shall be the inmates of the Fire; therein shall they abide. (2:30–39)

Adam was created in the world of decree as perfect, knowledgeable, and free, but his freedom was a gift for which he did not pay. God tested him to see what he would do with his freedom, so He said: "O Adam, dwell thou and thy wife in the garden, and eat therefrom plentifully wherever you will, but approach not this tree, lest you be of the wrong-doers." The tree he was prohibited from approaching was himself in the

---

26. *Iblis* is Satan or the Devil.

hidden meaning *(batin)*, and his wife in the apparent meaning *(zahir)*. He did not exercise his freedom properly, that is, by electing to follow the order of God rather than that of himself. As he elected himself rather than his Lord, and disobeyed Him and had intercourse with his wife, so his freedom was withdrawn, since he failed to exercise it properly. He descended to where he received the penalty for his offense, and began to recover his freedom by paying for it, in order to make him appreciate it and not further abuse it. Freedom that is not earned is not appreciated or defended. God warned His beloved Mohamed against Adam's situation: "Be praised God the real King, do not hasten with the Qur'an before it is properly revealed to you, and say please Lord, give me more knowledge. We have entrusted Adam previously but he had forgotten, and We found that he lacked will power." (30:14–15)

"We have entrusted Adam" means that We made him promise to exercise his freedom properly and elect God always. "But he had forgotten and We found that he lacked will power," means he forgot our promise, and his will power failed him in maintaining the duty of freedom, when he succumbed before the temptation of his wife, and his own desire, thereby abusing his freedom, so We abridged it. "That is how We deal with the offenders." (77:18)

While Adam disobeyed his Lord in forgetfulness and weakness in resisting himself, Iblis disobeyed deliberately and arrogantly. God tells us his story:

> Call to mind when thy Lord said to the angels: I am about to create man from clay, and so when I have fashioned him in perfection, and have breathed into him of My Spirit, fall ye down in submission to him. So the angels submitted, all of them together. But Iblis did not. He behaved proudly, and was of those who disbelieved. God said: O Iblis, what hindered thee from submitting to what I had created with My two hands? Is it that thou art too proud, or art thou really above obeying My command? Iblis said: I am better than he. Thou hast created me of fire and him has Thou created of clay. God said: Then get out hence, for, surely, thou art rejected; and, surely, on thee shall be My curse till the Day of Judgment. He said: My Lord, then grant me respite till the day when they shall be raised. God said: Certainly thou art of the respited ones till the day of the known time. Iblis said: So by Thy Glory, I will, surely, lead them all astray, except Thy chosen servants from among them. God said: The truth is, and the truth alone I speak, that I will, certainly, fill Hell with thee and with those who follow thee, all together. (38:71–85)

Iblis was a worshiper, but he was arrogant, so he was veiled by himself from his Lord, and his worship was of no use. Iblis was also knowledge-able, but it was superficial *zahir* knowledge, unaccompanied by profound *batin* knowledge, so he was neither fearful of God nor intelligent. He swore by the Glory of God that he would mislead them all, and yet he is too arrogant to obey God. When he failed to be fearful of God, he insisted on his disobedience rather than repent and ask forgiveness. He asked for a reprieve in order to find the chance to tempt and mislead. He said: "My Lord, then grant me respite till the day when they shall be raised." When the Lord said: "Certainly thou art of the respited ones till the day of the known time," he responded: "So by Thy Glory, I will, surely, lead them all astray, except Thy chosen servants from among them." The last verse indicates his knowledge, because he knew that he could not influence God's saved and exempted worshipers. But his knowl-edge, as indicated above, is knowledge in *zahir* only, with no *batin* genuine piety. In contrast, Adam and Eve said: "Our Lord, we have wronged ourselves, and if Thou forgive us not and have not mercy on us, we shall surely be losers." (7:23)

In any case, all of these disobeyed the order of their Lord, thereby becoming low and ignorant, incompatible with a refined spiritual en-vironment. The weight of disobedience brought them down the ladder of evolution to the very bottom, referred to in the above-quoted verses as "fig," that is to say, the most abysmal depth. The order of descent was with Iblis first, followed by Eve and then Adam. In their new environ-ment, they were surrounded on all sides by evils, but they soon adapted to their new environment and almost forgot all their former perfection. God answered Iblis' request; He reprieved him until the day of resurrection, so he remained at the most abysmal depth, with no ascent, because he did not ask to ascend, but merely to be reprieved. God also answered Adam's and Eve's request, so they remained at the most abysmal depth only until they received the forgiveness and mercy they asked for when they dis-obeyed the order of their Lord. "God's mercy is close to those who do good." (7:57)

When reading in the above-mentioned verses of *Surat al-Tin* (that is, chapter 95)—"But those who believed and did good deeds shall have unlimited reward"—one may think that this exception means they were not reduced to the bottom of creation. This is wrong. In fact, this verse and the one preceding it give the meaning of the verses: "And there is not one of you but will come to it; that is an absolute imperative of your Lord. And We shall leave the wrongdoers therein, [humbled] on their knees."

(19:71–72) Thus, He saved Adam and Eve from the most abysmal depth, and their ascent began because of the forgiveness and mercy of God. Iblis was left behind because he refused to change.

God asks: "What makes them disbelieve in religion?" Religion means the reward, which is reciprocity (al-mu'awadah), that is, retribution (al-qasas), on which we said Islam based its essence (haqiqah) and its Shari'a, or law. This reference is designed to show us that man was reduced from the state of the best mold to the most abysmal depth, in accordance with the law of reciprocity (al-mu'awadah) and fair and just penalty.

God says: "Is God not the wisest of the rulers" in endorsement of the law of reciprocity (al-mu'awadah) and to remind us of its inherent wisdom.

FORGIVENESS FOR ADAM AND EVE

How was Adam forgiven? God had ordered the angels to submit to Adam and they obeyed. He also ordered Iblis to submit to Adam and he disobeyed. The angels obeyed the Legislative Decree, as they "disobey not God in what He commands them and do as they are commanded." (66:6) Iblis, however, disobeyed the Legislative Decree, but by that same disobedience he had in fact obeyed the Creational Decree, as he must do so [as it is the Will of God]. Submission [by the angels] means rendering the angels servants to Adam and rendering Iblis a servant, with a difference of degree between the two servitudes. The servitude of the angels is assistance in doing good and guidance to truth (al-haq) while the servitude of Iblis is guidance towards evil and misguidance from truth.

Adam is divided between good from above and evil from below, and in both cases he is proceeding to God. "And He conferred upon you benefits both apparent and latent." (31:20) The apparent benefits are the fortunes, and the latent benefits are the misfortunes. All of this is mercy, but the self shuns misfortune and takes confort in fortunes. God says: "Fighting is ordained to you, though it is repugnant to you, but it may be that you dislike a thing while it is good for you, and it may be that you like a thing while it is bad for you. God Knows and you do not know." (2:216) The whole problem is the lack of knowledge.

If you imagine the first human standing on the line which separates the animals from the human being, and you imagine him as the spearhead of evolution, then you will have imagined Adam, the successor to earth, at some stage of his ancient development. This was, however, a stage of transition which he entered with an unparalleled leap, resulting from accumulating a number of qualities stored during his long and bitter evolution. God expresses that leap by saying: "Then We transformed him in a different being" in the verses: "We have created man of an extraction of clay. Then We set him, a drop, in a secure receptacle. Then We created the drop into a clot, then We created of the clot a tissue, then We created of the tissue bones, and covered the bones with flesh, then We transformed him into a different being. So blessed be God, the best of creators." (23:12–14)

That leap is also expressed in God saying "and breathed into him from My Spirit", in the two revered verses: "When your Lord told the angels: I am making a human being of dry ringing clay of black mud wrought into shape. So, when I have fashioned him and breathed into him from My Spirit, you shall submit to him." (15:28–29) The phrase "when I have fashioned him" refers specifically to the evolutionary chain which began with water vapor, when the heavens and the earth were a single cloud, until the scene was set for the Lord's Spirit to be blown into it. As already mentioned, the Lord's Spirit is "the will to be free" which crowned "the will to live," thereby suddenly elevating man above other superior animals. The will to be free did not materialize suddenly out of nothing; rather it emerged after a long period of latency or dormancy. It is like butter that is produced by struggle from the milk of life. We already said that the will to be free wrestled with the will to live, and the mind is the outcome of their encounter.

The will to live emerged from the earth; heavenly elements persisted in this force, but were weaker than the earthly elements. The will to be free emerged from the earth also, but the elements of the heavens therein were strong. The will to be free impelled human beings to stand on their own two legs and to walk, thereby freeing the hands for tasks that had more to do with the mind. Man began to look around and so to see the sun, the moon, and the stars, and to walk in erect form and discover the earth, as well as the ways of heavens: "Is he who walks with his face down better guided, or he who walks erect, on a straight path?" (67:22)

Adam in the universe is divided between angels from above, and the abalisah (plural of Iblis, or devils) from below; so he is the barzakh, isthmus of the whole universe. As such, he is also the mind of the whole universe. God, be praised and elevated, is referring to him when He said: "He merged the two seas into a meeting with an isthmus so neither of them encroaches upon the other." (55:19–20). The two seas here are the sea of the superior spirits which are enlightened with obedience, and the sea of the inferior spirits which are darkened by disobedience.

Adam's mind itself is divided between "the will to live," which is the self, from below, and "the will to be free," which is the spirit from above. So the mind is an isthmus and God refers to it as such in the two verses quoted above. This is their hidden (*batin*) meaning, while Adam is their apparent (*zahir*) meaning.

The law of the self is to seek pleasure by all means, and to avoid pain by all means. It therefore obeys the Creational Decree but finds it difficult to obey the Legislative Decree, because this places limitations on the self. In this way the self somewhat resembles Iblis.

The law of the spirit is that of the permissible and the impermissible. It demands that the self abstain from immediate prohibited pleasure in anticipation of the delayed permissible pleasure, and in order to avoid the pain that follows from indulging in impermissible pleasure, whether such pain was immediate or postponed. The spirit therefore not only obeys the Creational Decree but also the Legislative Decree as well. In this way, the spirit somewhat resembles the angels.

Adam, at that primitive stage of his development, was told to eat from this, and not to eat from that. In other words, he was told what was permissible and impermissible, and if he could resist the temptation to do evil and abstain from what was prohibited, he could exercise his freedom properly, thereby deserving to have more freedom. God says: "Is the reward of goodness anything but goodness?" (55:60) The reward of doing good is actually multiplied out of the pure grace of God. Listen to Him saying: "Whoso does a good deed shall have ten times as much [reward]; but he who does an evil deed, shall be repaid only with the like of it; and they shall not be wronged." (6:160) The good deed may also be multiplied many times, or even indefinitely. Listen to Him, to be praised and elevated: "The example of those who spend their money in the cause of God is like a seed that produced seven spikes, in every spike one hundred seeds, and God multiplies for whomsoever He wishes. God is infinitely wise, infinitely knowledgeable." (2:261)

Here the single seed produced seven spikes, in every spike one hundred seeds, which is already multiplication by seven hundred. In addition the Qur'an said, "God multiplies for whomsoever He wishes," such as multiplication of seven-thousands, or seventy-thousands. When it says "God is infinitely wise and infinitely knowledgeable," He had gone beyond counting, into infinite abundance.

If Adam was, however, unable to resist, and he was weakened in the face of temptation and indulged in securing impermissible pleasure, he abused his freedom, and consequently rendered it liable to abridgment. If such abuse involved offending against the rights of the community, his freedom could be abridged in accordance with the law of reciprocity (al-mu'awadah) in Shari'a, and its verse is: "We have decreed in it [revelation] that a life for a life, an eye for an eye, a nose for a nose, an ear for an ear, a tooth for a tooth, and wounds are to be judged according to retribution (qasas), and he who condones, it shall be taken to his advantage, but they who do not apply what God has revealed are the unfair ones." (5:45)

If his abuse of his freedom affected only himself, his freedom would be abridged in accordance with the law of reciprocity (al-mu'awadah) at al-haqiqah level under the two verses: "Then whoso does an atom's weight of good will see it. And whoso does an atom's weight of evil will also see it." (99:7–8) One should not think, however, that the law of reciprocity in Shari'a was always according to the rules mentioned in the Torah, as confirmed by the New Testament, and finally approved and confirmed by the Qur'an. The law of reciprocity is, in fact, an evolving law that develops with the evolution of human society, and is influenced by the degree of precision of the human mind and its ability to simulate the law of al-haqiqah, which is its eternal source. The law of al-haqiqah has always been, and remains, infinitely precise, universal, and all-embracing.

The precision of the law of reciprocity (al-mu'awadah) in al-haqiqah, which is missed in several of its forms by the law of reciprocity in Shari'a, is recovered in that both sets of laws concur to curb the freedom of those who do not use this freedom properly while avoiding the imposition of multiple penalties for the same sin at the same level of punishment. Reciprocity (al-mu'awadah) at the level of haqiqah is, however, much more precise than at the level of Shari'a. Of the laws of reciprocity (al-mu'awadah) at the level of Shari'a, the four hudod [strictly prescribed penalties for the specified offenses] are the nearest to the level of al-haqiqah in precision. These are zina (extramarital sexual intercourse), qadhf (defamation by false accusation with a zina), sariqa (theft), and qat'-al-tariq (highway robbery). All these penalties are based on two principles: the sanctity of sexual relations and the sanctity of property rights. These were the first two laws established by primitive human communities, thereby making society itself possible. Following these hudod, in precision, is the hadd of intoxication, followed by qasas, the other laws of retribution, such as life for a life, and an eye for an eye.

Reciprocity *(al-mu'awadah)* strives to curb evil by punishing indulgent and excessive self-pleasure by a balanced amount of pain to educate and teach the self to moderate its conduct and refrain from excessive and indulgent pursuit of pleasure.

HOW WAS ADAM FORGIVEN?

He was forgiven by being permitted to err. This means that his freedom was not abrogated by subjecting him to guardianship forever. Unlike Iblis, Adam was allowed to redeem his freedom and practice it according to his ability.

Adam started to exercise his freedom, vacillating in so doing between right and wrong. When he exercised his freedom properly, he was given more. Conversely, when he abused his freedom, he had to bear the consequences and was penalized according to the principle of reciprocity *(al-mu'awadah)*, which is a punishment corresponding to the sin. This process was intended to stimulate the powers of the self, thereby making it increasingly worthy of exercising freedom properly in those areas in which it was previously abused.

However, even such punishment reveals God's divine compassion, as He rewards good deeds ten times over, and may multiply the reward into infinity; while evil deeds are penalized only to a degree equal to their gravity. God may also forgive bad deeds, or even replace them with good, and then multiply them into infinity. As He, be praised and elevated, says:

> And those who call not on any other god along with God, nor slay a living thing whose slaying God has forbidden except for a just cause, nor commit adultery—and he who does that shall meet the punishment of [his] sin; doubled for him shall be the punishment on the Day of Resurrection, and he will abide there in disgrace—except those who repent, and believe and do righteous deeds; for as to these, God will convert their evil deeds into good ones, and God is Most Forgiving, Merciful. (25:68–70)

Adam was inspired with divine words, thereby becoming the cause of his own redemption through forgiveness: "Then Adam learned from his Lord certain words [of prayer]. So He turned towards him with mercy.

Surely, He is oft-returning [with compassion, and is] Merciful." (2:37) Those words were: "Our Lord, we have wronged ourselves, and if Thou forgive us not, and have not mercy on us, we shall surely be losers." (7:23).

Adam received forgiveness after he became a rational human being. However, it took many ages for him to reach this advanced stage. God described this: "There has, certainly, been a time when man was not a thing worth mentioning. We have created man of clear water mixed with mud, and continued to test him until We made him able to hear and see. We have guided his path onto either being thankful or ungrateful." (76:1–3) This means that there was a long period when man was not responsible, because his mind did not exist yet. We have spoken of this before and noted that God conducted life in a semi-direct manner, from its first manifestation in water and clay and until it reached the stage of the mind, through the law of reciprocity (al-mu'awadah) in al-haqiqah, in accordance with the two verses: "Then whoso does an atom's weight of good will see it. And whoso does an atom's weight of evil will also see it." (99:7–8) This law operates always to promote good and eliminate evil by guiding life into the fold of God the Merciful.

This tasir, processing and evolution towards God from the time he (Adam) was "clear water mixed with mud" until he becomes a responsible human being, constituted forgiveness for Adam. What was Adam before that and how was he forgiven? Listen to the Qur'an: "We have created man from an extraction of clay. Then We set him, a drop, in a secure receptacle." (23:12–13) Before Adam became a drop mixed with clay [water mixed with mud], he was a particle of water vapor, which is the origin of life. As God tells us: "Do the infidels not see that the heavens and earth were a closed-up mass, then We opened them out? And We made of water every living being. Will they not then believe?" (21:30) This particle of water vapor is the origin of the extraction of clay. Adam was forgiven at this stage through this direct determination (al-tasir), compulsion by the Will, which prompted life towards God and incited it to be close to Him, so it evolved and developed. The law of this Divine Will is also the law of reciprocity (al-mu'awadah).

This forgiveness for Adam at its various levels is actually determinism (al-tasir). People are subjected to determinism from the level of the elements to the level of life, and from the level of primitive life to the level of advanced, refined and complex life, and then from this level to the level of collective freedom with the emergence of the mind; and [finally] from the level of collective freedom to the level of absolute individual freedom. Determinism (al-tasir) proceeds to this last level indefinitely, because it is proceeding to God in infinity (itlaq).

DETERMINISM IS ABSOLUTE GOOD

With the advent of the mind, the law of reciprocity (al-mu'awadah) in Shari'a began to emerge. At the beginning, it was less refined in comparison to the law of reciprocity in al-haqiqah, but it increasingly became more precise and refined as the mind was strengthened and matured. It is the transitory law, reflecting the evolving human will, which is seeking to coincide completely with the original law; and while attempting to reflect the Lord's will, it shall never succeed in doing so completely.

Man is manipulated from distance into closeness, from ignorance into knowledge, from plurality into unity, from evil to good, from the limited to infinity (itlaq), and from bondage to freedom.

Determinism, from its very beginning, was mercy in the form of justice. In fact, it is greater than justice—"since mercy is superior to justice"—as previously indicated.

Determinism is freedom as it is based on "intelligent" free action at a certain level. Whoever exercises his freedom properly shall have more freedom, thereby rising higher through experience and practice. When freedom is not properly exercised, the sinner bears the consequences in accordance with a wise law that aims at improving his ability to exercise his freedom properly. In this way, man is manipulated from determinism (al-tasir) to free will (al-takhir), because he is free whenever he exercises his discretion properly, at the intellectual, verbal, and practical levels.

There is Hadith qudsi, which reports what God said to the Prophet David:[27] "Oh David, you will and I [God] will and there can be only what I will. If you surrender to what I will, I shall grant you what you will, and if you refuse to surrender to what I will, I shall make you suffer in what you will and, in the end, there can only be what I will." God settled the question from the beginning by saying that "there can be only what I will," thereby showing that only God's will is effective.

When He said, "If you surrender to what I will, I shall grant you what you will," He indicated that the will of the human being shall be effective

---

27. As explained in note 4 of this chapter, in a Hadith qudsi, such as this one, the Prophet, peace be upon him, reports what has been revealed to him in his own words, while the Qur'an is the exact text of the revelation, verbatim.

if he chooses God. If you ask: Can one choose God? the answer is that one cannot choose Him except insofar as God grants him the choice. God says "they learn nothing of His knowledge except what He wishes them to learn." (2:255) God wishes for us at every moment to learn more of His Knowledge; hence the reference, "Every day He [reveals Himself] in a fresh state." (55:29) In this way He continuously reveals Himself to His creatures so that they may know Him. His day is not twenty-four hours, but rather the time unit of such revelation in which a second might be divided into one billion parts of a second, to the extent that time itself almost ceases to be time. All of this is in accordance with the ability God has granted human beings to receive from Him. Since the ability to receive from God is subject only to God's wisdom, the limitation itself becomes freedom and the constraint becomes liberty. It is because of this absolute mercy that we have come to feel that we have an independent will, and this feeling obliges us to exercise this free will in a proper manner.

To exercise the free will properly is to choose God alone. If we do this with absolute certainty in thought, speech, and action, He shall grant us more free will. If we misuse our free will by choosing something other than God, He shall abridge our freedom in order to teach us how to exercise it properly in the future. The proper exercise of our freedom is a gift from Him, while our misuse is manifestation of His wisdom, namely, to prepare the place for receiving the gift. All of this takes place with such subtlety that it neither disturbs us nor does it nullify our existence.

We choose ourselves instead of God through our ignorance, but such ignorance is not permanent, and we move out of it and into more knowledge at every moment. One may ask, why were we not created knowledgeable to avoid the evils of ignorance, abuse of freedom, and the consequent penalty? The answer is that the penalty is the price we pay for freedom, because freedom is responsibility and responsibility is personal commitment to undertake the consequences of action, whether right or wrong.

God created some creatures who are knowledgeable and unable to make mistakes, but they are not free, and are therefore imperfect, namely, the angels. God preferred human beings over angels because of their ability to do right or wrong. In other words, their ability to learn. To this the Prophet refers: "If you do not make mistakes and then repent, God shall replace you by other people who make mistakes and then repent, whence they are forgiven." So it is as if the sinners who repent are the focus of God's perspective of the universe, because in that way they become free, absolutely free, and absolute freedom is the quality of God the Magnificent.

Every limited being is bound to become not only free, but even absolutely free, and every ignorant being is bound to become not only knowledgeable but even absolutely knowledgeable. God says: "O man, you are toiling along toward your Lord, and you shall meet Him." (84:6) He also says: "Did you think that We have created you in vain, and that you would not be brought back to Us?" (23:115) Meeting God and returning to Him is not done by covering distances, but rather by bringing qualities [of the slave] closer to the qualities [of the Lord]. That is why we have affirmed that determinism (al-tasir) is absolute good. It is, in fact good, both immediately and in the long run.

There shall be a time when ignorance will end, due to the grace of God through determinism (al-tasir). The Prophet refers to this when he said:

> "Had you depended on God properly and completely, He would have supported you the way He supports birds, and you would have learned all that there is to learn, which nobody did. The Companions said: Not even you. And the Prophet replied: Not even I. They said: We did not think the prophets fell short on anything. And he replied God is too great and important for anyone to know all that He can teach."

When there is less ignorance and more knowledge, there will be less evil, and the punishment will be suspended for those subject to it, in that area which has come under their knowledge.

Punishment is not the rule in religion, it is merely a transitional necessity accompanying the imperfect beginning, and prompting it up the ladder of evolution, until we learn enough to do without punishment. At that point punishment will be removed and the self shall emerge in its glory.

Every self is bound to emerge from the suffering of hell and go into paradise. Such a period may be long or short, depending upon the need of each for the experience. But for every fate there is a fixed duration, and for every such fixed duration, there has to be an end.

It is therefore a complete mistake for anyone to think that punishment in hell never ends, as he thereby makes evil the rule in the universe, which it is not. If punishment is eternal, it would be the vengeance of a grudging soul, totally lacking in wisdom. And God is absolutely free from this.

AL-QADA', PREDESTINATION AND AL-QADAR, FATE

The secret of fate (al-qadar) is the fine end of predestination (al-qada'), and God referred to this in the verse: "We have created everything for its time (bi-qadar), and Our Decree is but a unit, like the blink of an eye." (54:49–50) Predestination is this decree, which is a unit outside time and space, as indicated by the phrase "like the blink of an eye." Fate is the execution of predestination and its projection into time and space, gradually, slowly, and in an evolutionary process.

Predestination and fate are also referred to in another verse: "And God effaces and establishes what He Wills, and with Him is the source of all commandments." (13:39) The phrase "and God effaces and establishes what He Wills" refers to fate; in other words, it refers to evolution through successive forms of beings. We have already mentioned the fact that life evolves through various forms, seeking to become as stable in form as it is in essence, a pursuit continued into infinity. The phrase "and with Him is the source of all commandments" refers to predestination, which is the secret of fate.

Reference to predestination and fate is also made in the verse, "We have the stores for everything, but We release only in accordance with predetermined fate." (15:21) The phrase, "We release only in accordance with predetermined fate" refers to fate, while the phrase, "We have the stores for everything" refers to predestination, that is to say, the secret of fate.

Fate is a stage of duality where there is good and evil, knowledge and ignorance, but predestination is a unitary stage, where evil ceases to exist, and only absolute good remains, which is with God in infinity (itlaq). This is what is known to our friends [the sufis] as the secret of fate. But they did not speak of this, because for them it was improper to disclose it in view of hukm al-waqt, the dictates of the time, and in compliance with proper discipline.

Every creature has two precedents (sabiqah): one in predestination (al-qada') and another in fate (al-qadar). The precedent in predestination is absolute good for all creatures, while the precedent in fate is either good or evil, and it is concealed from people, although it may be indicated by events, which is the state of the particular individual in everyday life, whether good or evil. Knowledge of the individual's precedent sabiqah is not concealed from those with insight into the defects of observance of Shari'a in daily life. God had already sent messengers to regulate life through detailing the Shari'a, and concealed the precedent of each person in His preserved tablet, thereby casting the burden on His creation and obliging them to observe the Shari'a's permissions and proscriptions "so that people may have no plea against God after [the coming of] Messengers." (4:165)

God said: "And they said if the Gracious [God] had so willed, we should not have worshiped them [idols]. They have no knowledge whatsoever of that. They do nothing but conjecture." (43:20) They do not know what the will of the Gracious God is because it is concealed from them, but they do know His law—Shari'a, and its directive to worship no one but God. "They do nothing but conjecture" because they do not refer all things in their everyday lives to God, and they only refer to Him those matters pertaining to their worship, because of a relative lack of faith in the next life.

When the self discovers the secret of fate and is certain that God is pure good, it shall resort to Him, and accept Him, surrender and submit, thereby becoming liberated from fear and achieving peace within itself, and with other beings and things, purifying all thoughts of evil, preventing the tongue from hurting others, and refraining from assaulting others. The self also realizes its own unity, thereby becoming pure good, naturally disseminating the sweetness of good qualities like a flower disseminating good scent.

Here the heart prostrates, forever, at the threshold of the first stage of servitude [to God], where the slave ceases to be manipulated and becomes free, because determinism has taken him where he is honored by delivering him to freedom of choice. He has obeyed God until God obeyed him in reciprocity for his deed. He begins to live the Life of God, know His Knowledge, will his will, enjoy His Ability, and to become God.

God has no form for man to assume, and no end for man to reach, but man becomes God in the sense of continuing to be, by renewing his full intellectual and emotional life every moment, in accordance with God's description of Himself: "Every day He [reveals Himself] in a fresh state." (55:29) This is the objective of worship. The Prophet summed it up in his directive: "Adopt the qualities of God; my Lord is on the straight path." God also said: "Be of the Lord because you teach the Book and because you study [it]." (3:39)

With respect to these individuals, God said: "They shall have whatever they wish with their Lord, as that is the reward of the well-doers." (39:43) The phrase "They shall have whatever they wish" means they become free; and the phrase "with their Lord" means that they are in the stage of servitude to God, as only the slave can be with the Lord. The phrase "that is the reward of the well-doers" refers to those who exercise their absolute freedom properly by using it in achieving full servitude to God. As God said: "And I have created jinn (spirits) and people for no reason except that they may worship Me." (51:56)

This is the area of individualities, with Shari'a being Shari'a fardiyah, the law of the individual, and God Himself calling to Himself, where the slave faces the Lord, with no intermediaries, no veils, neither of darkness nor of light. Here, worship practice is to practice servitude to God, and action is to beware of the precedent (sabiqah) and to regulate one's life accordingly, until the balance is perfect. The slave of God at this stage is trying to be to his Lord God as the Lord is to him. This is what God meant: "Hold the balance at equilibrium and do not tilt the balance." (55:9) So if the slave is present with his Lord in exactly the same way the Lord is present with the slave, the balance is at equilibrium. But that is an infinite pursuit, never to be achieved exhaustively.

Here we may briefly refer to the practical value of worship. When the slave faces the Lord with no intermediaries, this means a meeting of the transitory with the eternal without any veil. The transitory here means the mind, while the eternal is the heart, also known as the unconscious or subliminal mind. The veils are corpses of wishes suppressed on the surface of the unconscious, due to ancient inherited fears at the beginning of human existence. This is the rust referred to in the verse: "Nay, but that which they have earned is rust upon their hearts." (83:14)

An individual can never achieve absolute individual freedom as long as he is divided within himself, with one part at war with the other. He must restore unity to his being, so that he may be at peace with himself, before he can attempt to be at peace with others. One cannot give what he does not have. One can be at peace with himself when the conscious is not in conflict and opposition with the unconscious. When unity between the two is established, there shall be wholesomeness of the heart and clarity of thought. At that point, full intellectual and emotional life is achieved, and this is the higher form of life.

Unification of the faculties within one's being is achieved when one thinks as he wishes, speaks as he thinks, and acts as he speaks. This is what the Qur'an demands of all of us when God says: "O believers, why do you say what you do not do? It is most hateful to God that you say what you do not do." (61:2–3).

The conflict between the conscious and the unconscious is resolved only through understanding the dissension that exists between the individual and the community, and between the individual and the universe.

We have already shown Islam's superiority in understanding and resolving these dissensions. The need to understand properly the relationship between the individual and the community, and between the individual and the universe, is derived from a practical need for a valid and single process by which the individual may achieve absolute individual freedom.

Scholars who believe that to admit determinism (al-tasir) is a negative attitude are mistaken. This is not true. The concealment of what is predetermined by fate (al-qadar) and revelation of what is required by Shari'a obliges man to try his best to observe Shari'a's directives and proscriptions, and then accept what may be predetermined by God out of reliance on God, and trust in Him. As the Prophet said: "God ordained perfection for everything, so if you kill, then kill well, and if you slaughter, then slaughter well; one must sharpen his knife and slay his subject comfortably."

In fact, performing one's immediate duty in the best manner possible is the most positive attitude, "because God ordained perfection for everything," while also accepting the result whatever it may be, without losing heart when one fails and without exulting in joy when one succeeds. God is educating and disciplining us when He says:

> There befalls no calamity either in the earth or in your persons but is recorded in a Book before We bring it into being. Surely, that is easy for God. Thus it is so that you may not grieve over what is lost to you nor exalt because of that which He has bestowed upon you. And God loves not any conceited boaster, such as are niggardly and enjoin others to be niggardly. And whoso turns his back should know that God is Self-Sufficient, Worthy of all praise. (57:22–24)

CONCLUSION

In conclusion, the relationship between the individual and the universe is neither one of animosity and hostility, nor of endless strife and struggle.

Man is both the fruit of the universe and its elite, a king who must rule wisely, competently, and fairly. God, in His grace, has permitted man to be His viceregent,[28] and He is preparing him for that viceregency by education and wise guidance. Man's ignorance caused him to imagine that

28. Reference here is to the Qur'an (2:30) where God describes man as His viceregent.

he was the object of more or less constant hostility, so he began to fight pointless battles and develop antagonisms needlessly. He cannot achieve his viceregency until he outgrows these animosities, see that he is above antagonism, and rid his heart of all but love and compassion. God loves all creation: gases, liquids, stones and metals, plants, animals, man, angels and demons. He created all through the Will, which is love.[29] Man cannot be God's viceregent over His creation until his heart is large enough to love all creation, in all its forms, and dispose of it wisely and constructively.

The greatest obstacle to love is fear. It has been the source of all defects in human behavior throughout the ages. Man will not deserve to be God's viceregent on earth, or to rule properly over his kingdom, if he is afraid. And Islam is the only effective means to liberate man from his fears. Through Islam man comes to peace with himself, his Lord and all beings and matter. God says: "Oh believers, come into peace (silm) all of you, and follow not the footsteps of Satan; surely, he is your open enemy." (2:208). Silm means Islam [submission to God] as well as peace. "Follow not the footsteps of Satan" who incites animosity and hatred amongst you. Reference to animosity is made in the phrase "he is your open enemy."

---

29. The Arabic word for will is *iradah,* and the word for love is *raydah.* The author finds it significant that the two words share their root and appear to be linguistically related.

4

Islam

We have discussed the relationship between the individual and the community and between the individual and the universe in philosophy and Islam, seeking to discover in Islam the answers that we have failed to find in philosophy. Now that God has granted these answers to us, we turn to discover the ground on which we stand.

WHAT IS ISLAM?

"*Aslam*" means surrendered and submitted. Islam, in essence [that is, according to its basic nature] is surrender and submission. God explains this when He says "Do they seek other than the Religion of God, to Whom all those in heaven and earth have already surrendered, whether willingly or unwillingly, and to Whom they shall return?" (3:83) Religion in this context means practical life, behavior and attitudes, the way or path. The Religion of God means the way of God with His creation, which is the essence of things.

The essence of things is to submit to God, "to Whom all those in heaven and earth have already surrendered, whether willingly or un-willingly, and to Whom they shall return." Islam, in this sense, is the religion of all creatures, including man, at the beginning, in the end, and in between.

God's mercy did not wish that all creatures should submit without free will. Rather, and in the most subtle way, God permitted the vanguard of all creatures, namely man, to believe that he is different from other creatures. This illusion is the cause of man's suffering in the short-run and also of his ultimate happiness. The illusion came with the will to be free granted by God. To this God refers when He says: "We have offered the trust to the heavens and the earth and the mountains, but they all refused to take it, and were fearful of it. Man accepted it; he is surely unfair and ignorant." (33:72) The phrase "he was surely unfair and ignorant" is actually praise in the form of blame. It is because of their acceptance of this entrustment that human beings were honored. God says: "We have honored the children of Adam and we carried them by land and sea, granted them good livelihood, and have exalted them far above many of those We have created." (17:70)

God tells us of man's illusion that he is different from other creatures when He says: "Did you not see that to God submits whosoever is in the heavens, and whosoever is in the earth, and the sun, and the moon, and the stars, and the mountains, and the trees, and the beasts, and many people? But there are many who deserve punishment. And whomsoever God disgraces, none can raise him to honor. Verily, God does what He pleases." (22:18)

The word "submits" has many meanings, including acquiescence to compulsion by the Will. Acquiescence occurs in man in the same way it occurs in inorganic matter. The term also has the meaning of prostration in worship, which God meant when He said "and many people." These are they who prostrated their bodies in worship. The second part refers to those who refuse to worship: "there are many who deserve punishment," not because they did not acquiesce to the compulsion of the Will, since they in fact did that; but it was not accepted from them as they are required to prostrate themselves in worship and they failed to do so, thus deserving punishment.

Submission also means submission in servitude to God, but this has never been accomplished exhaustively and shall never be, because, like Godhood (al-rubwbiah) it is infinite. But the pioneers of humanity, namely, the prophets, have achieved varying degrees of such submission. The phrase, "These are two disputants who dispute concerning their Lord" (22:19), which refers to every worshiper and indicates the division within the human personality into the apparent (zahir) and the hidden (batin), affirms that submission in full servitude to God has never been complete. The human self shall remain forever so divided, as it is of a dual nature, while complete servitude remains the domain of the indivisible self, an infinite pursuit. [1]

1. As explained above, this is the direction of unlimited and infinite development, as one is seeking infinite, or absolute servitude. Whatever is achieved, ceases to be absolute, and a fresh goal is set up, on the horizon, for one to strive to achieve.

Submission in worship is a means to the submission of servitude, because with it man removes the illusion, thereby releasing himself from imprisonment to freedom, from ignorance to knowledge, from unhappiness to happiness when he submits voluntarily to the compulsion of the Will, with the intelligence, understanding, and appreciation that distinguish him from inorganic matter. It is to this supreme submission that God refers in the subtle verse, "Who has a better religion than he who submits himself entirely to God intelligently and knowingly and follows Abraham's perfect creed. God has taken Abraham for a special friend." (4:125) The subtlety here is in the phrase "intelligently and knowingly," which is the key to the verse. It is also the key to the verse which says, "And he who submits himself to God, intelligently and knowingly, has grasped the secure handle, and to God everything shall return." (31:22) The phrase "intelligently and knowingly" is the key to both verses, because all inorganic matter also submits itself to God, but not intelligently and knowingly. Hence, there is no point in its submission, because it is merely in accordance with the Will of God, falling short of His approval, which is reserved for human beings alone and for whose benefit God had sent the messengers, as indicated above.

Islam in this sense is the religion of humanity which accommodates human illusion, inspired by the will to be free, until man is gradually enlightened through realistic wisdom to eventually achieve intelligent Islam.

Islam, as the religion of humanity, developed with the evolution of the mind, and accompanied the maturing mind in its long evolution from a primitive beginning to its wise and refined end.

Islam, as the religion of humanity, is also the Religion of God mentioned in the above quoted verse: "Do they seek other than the Religion of God, to Whom all those in heaven and earth have already surrendered, whether willingly or unwillingly, and to Whom they shall return?" Islam as the religion of humanity is also described in the verse, "And he who seeks a religion other than Islam, it shall not be accepted of him, and in the hereafter he shall be among the losers." (3:85) The phrase "and in the hereafter he shall be among the losers" means that man's attempts shall fail; thus he will be finally reduced to submission, after other failed endeavors. Another verse has the same connotation: "Surely, the true religion for God is Islam. And those who were given the Book disagreed only [out of envy] after knowledge had come to them. And whoso denies the Signs of God, then surely, God is quick at reckoning." (3:19).

The word "with" [God] does not refer to either time or place, because God is not contained in either time or place. Rather it means "infinite perfection." Islam as the religion of humanity ultimately parallels Islam as the religion from the elements, and demands the same degree of submission from both, although humanity must have awareness and understanding of this submission, an infinite pursuit.

The phrase "those who were given the Book disagreed only [out of envy] after knowledge had come to them" means, in one sense, that they differed only in their laws. In fact, religion is basically one, and only the laws differ. God says: "Mankind was one community, then God raised prophets as bearers of good tidings and as warners, and sent down with them the Book containing the truth to adjudicate between people wherein they differed." (2:213) They were a single nation with their primitive ignorance, and God "sent down with them [the prophets] the Book" means *"la ilah ila-Allah"*2 together with the law best suited to their community and for their worship. Then [with the law] appeared the difference, and hence the Qur'an says "to adjudicate between people wherein they differed."

Concerning the unity of religion, the Qur'an notes: "And to God belongs whatever is in the heavens and whatever is in the earth. And We have commanded those who were given the Book before you and [commanded] you also to fear God. But if you disbelieve, then [remember that] to God belongs whatever is in the heavens and whatever is in the earth, and God is Self-Sufficient, Praiseworthy." (4:131) The phrase "We have commanded those who were given the Book before you, and [commanded] you also to fear God" means We directed them as We directed you, to say *la ilah ila-Allah,* as this is the ultimate in fear of God. It is in fact the "expression of fear" indicated in the verse: "The infidels had in their hearts the zeal of ignorance, then God brought down His serenity upon His messenger, and upon the believers, and committed them to the expression of fear of God, and they deserved it, as it was their own, and God was knowledgeable of everything." (48:126) The expression of the fear of God is *la ilah ila-Allah,* hence the Hadith of the Prophet: "The best that I, and the prophets before me brought is *la ilah ila-Allah.*"

Again, on the unity of religion, God says: "He has ordained for you the Religion which He enjoined to Noah, and which We revealed to you, and what We enjoined to Abraham and Moses and Jesus: Establish Religion and do not disperse in it. It is very difficult for the infidels [to

2. This phrase literally means there is no god but God, that is, that God is the only Lord and Creator. In this context it refers to the confession of a monotheistic faith.

accept] what you invite them to [accept]. God chooses for Himself whom He pleases, and guides to Himself him who turns [to Him]." (42:13) The phrase "He prescribed for you religion which He enjoined to Noah" means He explained to you religion which He had decreed to Noah, which is also what He had decreed to Adam. In explaining it to you, He is also decreeing it to you now also. This does not mean the law, Shari'a, but rather the *twhid* upon which the Shari'a is based. This is so because, while *twhid* is one, Shari'a [the laws] varies, and also because He says: "Establish religion and be not divided therein. Hard upon the idolaters is that to which you call them." It is difficult for the idolaters who believe in plurality (polytheism) to be called to *tawhid* (monotheism). It is the manifestation of the *tawhid* into the law that renders the law liable to be contravened, because the individuals do not practice *tawhid* [in the abstract].

Islam as a religion began to appear with the first human being, as we have explained in the chapter on the relationship between the individual and the community. Islam ultimately endeavors to coincide with the Lord's Will, as we have also explained when speaking of the Creational Decree and Legislative Decree. Hence, it has a beginning and no end; because its end is with God: "Surely, the true religion with God is Islam."

This concept of religion appeared first in several early pagan beliefs, developed into more advanced beliefs, and finally resulted in the mono-theist religions with divinely inspired Books, that is, Judaism, followed by Christianity. The whole process was crowned with the coming of Mohamed and the revelation of the holy Qur'an.

This concept has a pyramid-like structure, with the bottom poly-theistic paganisms as its base, while its peak is with God, where there is absolute unity. It is obvious that the difference between religion at the "bottom" and the "top" is a difference of degree and not of essence.

This concept of religion evolved from earth in the same way life evolved between water and mud. It also continued to be divided between heaven and earth—inspired by heavenly forces to spiritual peaks and then reduced and moderated by earthly factors, thereby widening the base and lowering the peak. This widening of the base is the preparation for a new summit, higher than the previous one, in response to the next heavenly inspiration. Thus religion passed through stages of inspiration and re-lapse.

In this way this great concept continued to evolve up the ladder of perfection, like a wave moving between a crest and a trough, with each crest higher than the previous one, and every trough wider than the previous one also, until the earthly spirituality approached the threshold of heavens. Thus all divine revelation is now on earth, contained in the Qur'an but still awaiting implementation.

THE ISLAMIC TRINITY

With the coming of Moses, and the descent of the Torah upon the sons of Israel, the Islamic concept entered a new phase, the phase of the scriptural religions, namely Judaism, Christianity, and Islam—with the Torah for the Jews, the Gospel for the Christians and the Qur'an for the Muslims.

The new phase was distinguished by the unprecedented breadth of religious legislation. All laws are related to the Lord through divine revelation to Moses. Religious legislation revealed from the Single Lord aimed at regulating the life of society, in every large or small detail, and in a comprehensive fashion. For the first time in history, monotheistic belief merged with the regulative law on a wide scale. Then came Jesus with the New Testament, and the Islamic Trinity was completed with the sending of the Final Prophet [Mohamed]. The Qur'an relates the story:

> We have surely sent down the Torah wherein was guidance and light for the prophets who have submitted to God to judge by it the Jews, [as did] the godly people and those learned [in the Law] because they were required to preserve the Book of God, and [because] they were guardians over it. Do not fear people but fear Me, and do not sell My signs for a cheap price. Those who do not judge according to what God revealed are the infidels. We have decreed in it [revelation] that a life for the life, and eye for an eye, a nose for a nose, an ear for ear, a tooth for a tooth, and wounds are to be judged according to retribution (qasas) and he who condones, it shall be taken to his advantage, but they who do not apply what God has revealed are the unfair ones. And We caused Jesus, son of Mary, to follow in their footsteps, fulfilling that which was [revealed] before him in the Torah; and We gave him the Gospel which [contained] guidance and light, fulfilling that which was [revealed] before him in the Torah and a guidance and an admonition for the God-fearing. And let the people of the Gospel judge according to what God has revealed therein, and who judges not by what God has revealed are the sinful. And We have revealed to you the Book comprising the truth [and] fulfilling that which was [revealed] before it in the Book, and as a guardian over it. Judge, therefore, between them according to what God

has revealed, and follow not their evil desires [turning away] from the truth which you have received. For each of you We prescribed a [clear] Law and a [manifest] way. And if God had wished, He could have made [all] one people, but He [wishes] to try you by that which He has given you. Compete in doing good, to God all of you shall return, then He will inform you of that wherein you differed. (5:44–48).

Moses was sent in the thirteenth century B.C., when society was primitive and crude, the individual quarrelsome and bad tempered, with his jungle experience still fresh in his mind. So the Torah called upon him to be fair—in reciprocity—so that his law became that of a life for a life and an eye for an eye. But it also invited and tempted him to forgive, by saying, as reported in the Qur'an, "and he who condones it shall be taken to his advantage." That is to say, he who condones and gives away his right to take retribution against the aggressor, God shall compensate out of His Grace for the injury he had suffered. This is what the Qur'an meant when it said "containing guidance and light": the guidance is the law, and the light is the moral precepts above the law. Such moral precepts are the fine end of the law, going beyond legal obligation to the voluntary commitment of each individual on his own.

The Torah demanded retribution (gasas), with almost nothing else, because it is closer to the nature of the primitive human self, which was so much used to quarrelsomeness and aggression that it was too much to expect it to be fair, let alone to forgive. The sons of Israel always reverted from the clear path to which they were invited. At the peak of their religion, with Moses still amongst them and the victory God granted them against their enemy still fresh in their minds, they longed to worship the calf. As the Qur'an tells their story: "When they came upon a people who worshipped the idols, they said to Moses: 'Make us a god as they have gods'; and he replied: 'You are an ignorant people. The way of these people will end, and what they do is invalid. Do you want a god other the God who preferred you to everybody else?'" They kept silent, but were unconvinced and unbelieving. When Moses went to his appointment with his Lord and deputized his brother Aaron over his people, they took the calf as their lord, saying that this is your lord, the lord of Moses. As God said: "Could they not see that it cannot answer them, and had no power to do them either harm or good? Aaron had already told them, Oh my people, you have only been tried by means of [the calf]. And, surely the Gracious God is your Lord, so follow and obey me. They replied, We shall not cease to worship it until Moses returns to us." (20:89–91).

Many scenes in the Qur'an speak of the crudeness and coarseness of the Jews, and how they stayed on the ground every time spiritual advancement was asked of them. This is only natural in that ancient stage in development. Despite their condition, the Jews were the elites of humanity of their time: "God chose Adam and Noah and the family of Abraham and the family of Imran, above all other peoples [of the time]." (3:33) The Jews were the family of Abraham and the family of Imran; "they were descendants of one another, and God is All-Hearing, All-Knowing." (3:34).

In any case, the laws of the Torah were somewhat primitive, and the Jews, when applying those laws, did not entirely rid themselves of pagan influences from the time of their Egyptian [captivity], a factor that made their laws even more primitive.

Then came Jesus with the law that pulled people to the other extreme, a reaction to what prevailed previously. This is something every diligent worshiper experiences. At the beginning of undertaking diligent worship, one is locked up, as his spirit is covered with its darkness. As he begins to practice worship according to the methods of the Prophet Ahmad,[3] by fasting continuously for three days and two nights, or seven days and six nights,[4] while continuing the prayer, especially the night prayer of the last third of the night, the self which was locked in darkness is pulled to the other extreme. If this *Ahmadi* method is continued for a sufficient period, then the self becomes increasingly enlightened and liberated, yet continuing to fluctuate, like a pendulum, between flashes of enlightenment and darkness. The ideal is absolute equilibrium, but that is unattainable, as that is the state of "the eye deviated not, nor did [it] wander" (53:17).

This emergence of the trinity of the diligent worshiper reflects the trinity of the three religions: Judaism, Christianity, and Islam. In this way, the development of the individual human being parallels the history of human society as a whole. That is why Jesus came with excessive

3. The methods of the Prophet Ahmad are those of the Prophet Mohamed himself at a higher level of achievement in religious knowledge. These methods follow the personal example of the Prophet more closely, and in greater detail and accuracy. Ahmad is one of the names of the Prophet of Islam, used in Islamic *sufi* (mystic) literature to indicate his superior spiritual achievements.

4. While in normal religious fasting, a Muslim would fast all day and eat and drink at night, in this type of fasting, known as *syam samadi*, one continues to fast, day and night, for the full duration of the period of three, five, or seven days, as the case may be, as a religious exercise.

spirituality, in contrast to the excessive materialism of the Jews. Jesus told his disciplines: "Think not that I am come to destroy the law, or the prophets: I am not come to destroy, but to fulfill." (Matthew 5:17) This is what the Qur'an refers to in the above quoted verses: "And We caused Jesus, son of Mary, to follow in their footsteps, fulfilling that which was [revealed] before him in the Torah; and We gave him the Gospel which [contained] guidance and light, fulfilling that which was [revealed] before him in the Torah, and a guidance and an admonition for the God-fearing" (5:46). So Jesus fulfills what preceded him in the Torah, and his Gospel fulfills what preceded it in the Torah. As he said, he does not destroy, but fulfills, develops, and elaborates concepts not fully appreciated previously because of the dictates of the time and circumstances. Jesus advanced religious concepts and principles almost to the ultimate.

Listen to him teaching his disciples: "Ye have heard that it hath been said: An eye for an eye, and a tooth for a tooth. But I say unto you, that ye resist not evil; but whosoever shall smite thee on thy right cheek, turn to him the other also" (Matthew 5:38–39). Jesus came when the Romans exercised temporal authority over the Jews and when Jewish law was, consequently, in some respects inoperative. Hence, Jesus' message did not address the practical concerns of regulating the life of society, but merely advancing certain moral commandments. This feature was reenforced by the fact that Jesus did not live long. He survived for only three years after commencing his mission.

In fact, the law of the Jews is the law of Christians, as improved upon by Jesus. This fact is generally neither appreciated nor observed by Christians.

"And We gave him the Gospel which [contained] guidance and light." "Guidance" here also means the law, while "light" means the moral precepts above the law. The Gospel develops moral precepts further than does the Torah. That is why it made forgiveness its law, as directed by its Messenger. When Jesus Christ said, "Ye have heard that it hath been said: An eye for an eye, and a tooth for a tooth," he is referring to the most primitive form of religious law, which was lacking in spirituality. Then he added: "But I say unto you, that ye resist not evil; but whosoever shall smite thee on thy right cheek, turn to him the other also"; he is expressing the rule in its extreme form, which is excessive in spirituality.

Then with Mohamed came Islam, which represents an equilibrium between the two extremes of the lack and the excess. Of the three religions Islam achieves an equilibrium of the state of "the eye deviated not, nor did [it] wander" (referred to above) similar to that equilibrium that may be achieved within the powers inherent in the human being. God says on this point: "And thus have We made you a middle nation, so that you may stand in testimony upon people, and the Messenger [of God] stands in testimony upon you" (2:143). "Middle nation" means a nation in between the two extremes of lack and excess of spirituality. To "stand in testimony upon people" means to have all the qualities common to all people. The verse: "Guide us to the straight path, [which is] the path of those on whom You have bestowed your favors, [not that of] those who have incurred your anger or those who have gone astray." (1:6–7). The straight path is the middle course between the two extremes, one deserv-ing of God's anger because of its lack of spirituality, and the other gone astray because of its extreme and excessive spirituality. "Those on whom You have bestowed [your] favors" are the Muslims, as indicated by the verse: "Today I have perfected your religion for you, completed My grace upon you, and sanctioned Islam as your faith." (5:3)

Since Islam, as brought by Mohamed, is in the equilibrium between Judaism and Christianity, the Qur'an also contains the qualities of both Judaism and Christianity. For example, "The penalty for evil is an equal evil, but he who forgives and reforms, his reward is upon God, He does not love the unfair ones." (42:40) The phrase: "the penalty for evil is an equal evil" corresponds to the statement in the Torah, as reported by Jesus, "An eye for an eye, and a tooth for a tooth." The Qur'anic statement, however, is not identical to the Torah, as it involves a step forward in making the penalty of retribution (qasas) repulsive, thereby setting the scene for forgiveness by describing retribution against an aggressor as "evil." The phrase "but he who forgives and reforms, his reward is upon God, he does not love the unfair ones" is similar to Jesus' statement "But I say unto you, That ye resist not evil; but whosoever smite thee on thy right cheek, turn to him the other also," although it is not quite identical to it either. The Qur'anic verse calls for an even greater degree of forgiveness. This Qur'anic phrase "he who forgives and reforms, his reward is upon God" corresponds to Jesus' saying "Love your enemies, bless them that curse you, do good to them that hate you, and pray for them which despitefully use you, and persecute you." (Matthew 5:44)

The fact that Islam achieves an equilibrium between the beginning and the end [Judaism and Christianity], partaking of the qualities of both ends, makes Islam itself of two ends: one end closer to the beginning [Judaism] and the other closer to the end [Christianity]. This is true of every equilibrium between two points, such as a child that inherits the qualities of both parents. Such inheritance may vary in proportion, but the qualities of both parents are always present, in one degree or another.

This clearly valid conclusion has far-reaching consequences for the future of Islamic thought. It means that Islam, as revealed in the Qur'an, is not one message, but two: one at the beginning closer to Judaism, and the other at the end closer to Christianity. The Prophet delivered both messages, by delivering the Qur'an and living his exemplary life. While detailing and elaborating the first message in the Shari'a, he left the second message unelaborated, except for those aspects which are common to both the first and the second messages and which would remain an integral part of the second message as well. This is especially so with respect to *'ibadat* (worship practices) except for the specific portions of *zakah*.[5]

---

5. As explained below, the author is not proposing a reduction in the proportions of *zakah*, but rather the establishment of a socialist system where the poor have what they need as of right, and not as a matter of charity. It remains open, and highly commendable, for every individual to give away as much as possible in exercise of his religious duty.

5

The First Message

The First Message of Islam has been elaborated through specific legislation. It is the message of al-Mu'minin, who must be distinguished from al-Muslimin, though the difference between the two is only of degree and not of essence.[1] Every *mu'min* is not necessarily a *muslim*, but every *muslim* is (in the sense explained above) necessarily a *mu'min* as well.

Islam is both a beginning and an end. Ideas, as also time and place, can be considered spiral in nature. The worshiper, aspiring to the higher levels of Islam, ascends a spiritual spiral, by which after each cycle, when the beginning of the cycle is reached, a new cycle begins at a superior level. The Islamic spiral consists of seven cycles beginning with *al-islam*, followed by *al-iman*, *al-ihsan*, *'ilm al-yaqin*, *'ilm 'ayn al-yaqin*, *'ilm haqq al-yaqin*, and finally, at the end of the cycle, *al-islam*.[2]

The people to whom the First Message of Islam was addressed are, strictly speaking, al-Mu'minin. The term *al-Muslimin,* as they are often called, may apply to them in the sense of initial Islam, but certainly not in the sense of final, ultimate, Islam.

The Qur'anic verse, "Surely, the true religion for God is Islam" (3:19) clearly refers to ultimate Islam and not Islam in its initial stage. Islam, in its initial stage, was sometimes claimed by hypocrites who embraced Islam to preserve their own lives while deeply resenting the Prophet and his Companions. Such men were tolerated because the Prophet said: "I have

1. This distinction has been discussed in the introductions to the third and fourth editions of this book.
2. On these terms see the Introduction to the Third Edition above.

been instructed to fight people until they declare that *la ilah ila-Allah* and that Mohammed is the Messenger of God, undertake the prayers, pay *zakah* (alms). Once they do they will have secured their lives and property, unless they violate the law. And I leave their sincerity to be judged by God." Islam developed between the two towns of Mecca and Medina, beginning in Mecca [around 610 A.D.]; when it failed to gain acceptance there, the Prophet migrated to Medina [in 622 A.D.], where Islam succeeded. It could not possibly have been accepted in Mecca, and so it was in fact rejected—"And these are similitudes which We set forth for mankind, but only the knowledgeable understand them." (29:43)[3]

It was not ultimate Islam that succeeded then, but rather Islam at the level of *al-iman*. The Qur'an itself is divided into two parts: one of *al-iman* and the other of *al-islam*, in the sense that the former was revealed in Medina, while the latter was revealed earlier in Mecca. Each class of texts has its own distinguishing features, reflecting the fact that the Medinese Qur'an pertains to the stage of *al-iman*, while the Meccan Qur'an pertains to the stage of *al-islam*. For example, those parts of the Qur'an which use the phrase "O believers," with the exception of *Surat al-Haj* (chapter 22), are Medinese, as are verses where the hypocrites are mentioned or reference is made to *jihad*.

The Meccan Qur'an, on the other hand, is distinguished by several features. For example, every chapter which mentions prostration, or opens with the alphabetical letters, is Meccan with the exception of *Surat al-Baqarah* and *al'Imran* (chapters 2 and 3), which are Medinese. Again, any chapter which uses the phrases: "O, mankind," or "O, children of Adam" is Meccan, with the exception of *Surat al-Baqarah* and *al-Nisa'* (chapters 2 and 4).

These exceptions are due to the overlap between the phases of *al-iman* and *al-islam*. As mentioned above, every *mu'min* is a *muslim* of the initial type, but not necessarily *muslim* of the ultimate type, while every *muslim* of the ultimate type is, and continues to be, a *mu'min*.

The Meccan and the Medinese texts differ, not because of the time and place of their revelation, but essentially because of the audience to whom they are addressed. The phrase "O believers" addresses a particular nation, while "O, mankind" speaks to all people. The verses "You have received a messenger from amongst yourselves who is deeply distressed by

3. The author is referring here to the notion of *hukm al-waqt*, the dictates of the time, religion's response to concrete social and economic circumstances, which is central to the author's own thesis for the evolution of Islamic law.

your suffering, cares for you, and he is tender and merciful to the believers" (9:128) in contrast to the verse "God is truly tender and merciful upon mankind" (2:143) demonstrate the different audiences to which the Qur'an speaks,[4] that is, the difference between a *mu'min* and a *muslim*.

The hypocrites were mentioned for the first time in Medina, during the ten years of revelation, but never during the Meccan thirteen years of revelation, because there were no hypocrites in Mecca. People were either believers or nonbelievers in Mecca where, since there was no compulsion, the verses of persuasion prevailed. "Propagate the path of your Lord in wisdom and peaceable advice, and argue with them in a kind manner, your Lord is more Knowledgeable of those who stray from His path, and He is more Knowledgeable of the guided ones." (16:125) Many other verses [of the Mecca period] also require the use of peaceful persuasion.

After the migration to Medina, and the abrogation of the verses of peaceful persuasion, the verses of compulsion by the sword prevailed—for example, "And when the forbidden months have passed, slay the idolaters wherever you find them and take them [captive], and beleaguer them, and lie in wait for them at every place of ambush. But if they repent and observe prayer and pay the *zakah*, then leave their way [free]. Surely God is Most Forgiving, Merciful." (9:5) Under this threat of violence some people had to seek refuge by concealing one view and declaring another, thereby introducing hypocrisy into the Islamic community.

The reference to *jihad* and the elaboration of its rules is a characteristic feature of Medinese Qur'an and needs no further explanation.

Prostration, as mentioned above, is one of the distinguishing features of the Meccan Qur'an, because prostration [genuine submission to God] is inherent in *al-islam* but not in *al-iman*. The Hadith says: "The slave is closest to his Lord when he is prostrating." The Qur'an also says: "Prostrate and draw nearer [to God]." (96:19) Prostration is an important step in developing toward a higher level of servitude [to God].

Another distinguishing Meccan feature is the opening of chapters with letters of the alphabet. Although this feature is extremely important to the essence of the Qur'an, we must limit ourselves here to discussing its relevance to the distinction between the two messages of Islam.

Fourteen letters, or half the letters of the Arabic alphabet, are used in Qur'anic chapters openings. These are used to open twenty-nine chapters

4. In the first verse tenderness and mercy are confined to the believers, while in the second verse they are conferred upon the whole of mankind.

in fourteen formations, namely: *alif lam mim, alif lam mim sad, alif lam ra',*
alif lam mim ra, kaf ha' ya' 'ayn sad, ta' ha', ta' sin mim, ta' sin, ya' sin, sad,
ha' mim, ha'mim 'ayn sin qaf, qaf, nun. All these formations are followed by
verses indicating that they are the Qur'an. The clearest example of this is
where God says in chapter 2:1–2: "*Alif lam mim.* That is the Book,
without any doubt, for the guidance of the God fearing." These two verses
are sometimes read while pausing at a different point, making it mean the
following: "*Alif lam mim.* That is certainly the Book which contains
guidance for the God fearing."[5] This, however, is not essential here, since
under both methods of reading the "Book" refers to *"Alif lam mim."*

The letters of the alphabet have developed since ancient times from
extremely primitive forms, to their present form. Man's need to write and
communicate preceded his need for customs regulating the daily life of
society. These customs, as we explained earlier, curtailed the whims of
the individual and commanded respect for certain limitations.

The need for communication and transmission of ideas was dictated
by the need to live in society. Animals felt the need for communal
coexistence, but only man truly achieved this, because of his ability to
communicate. This was accomplished through imitating the sounds of
elements and living beings, and man's upright stature and freed hands and
head as well as his developed vocal chords were particularly useful in this
regard. This faculty of imitation, perfected by man, was the origin of
language and writing, and their further development and refinement,
from their simple and naive beginnings, up to the near perfect means of
the present day.

This faculty of imitation granted by God to man is also the basis of
learning and perfection. In imitation there must first be absorption of the
original, then harmonization of the means of imitation, that is hands,
head, face or eyes—together with the mind. Such endeavors accomplish a
certain coordination or unity of the mind and body. Such unification of
mind and body is not yet complete, but continues to develop.

Although a need for writing emerged at about the same time as the
need for spoken language, it was not as urgent. For a long time gestures
sufficed. Writing started with drawings of objects and animals, or illustra-
tions of incidents for those who had not been present. Drawing a picture
of an animal was part of the hunting ritual, which also related to the

5. The slight difference in translation is intended to bring out the effect of the
difference in the point of pausing. Such difference, however, does not affect the point the
author is making in the text.

rituals of faith and worship. Perhaps the hunter believed he would possess the animal in hunting if he possessed its picture in his cave, believing in some type of transference between form and spirit.

The process developed in that the artist began to draw only part of the animal he wished to express, for example, the head of a bull instead of the entire body. Such refinements continued until the present letters of the alphabet emerged, after a long and slow development.

The number of letters of the alphabet varies from one language to another. These are twenty-eight in the Arabic language, beginning with *al-alif* and ending with *al-ghayn*.[6] This makes Arabic the most perfect language in this regard, as we will explain below.

Counting underwent a similar development. It was suggested and assisted by observation of the fingers and toes. The number of ten became the basis of counting, since the process started by using the ten figures. Numbers, as we know them today, did not emerge until after a very long process of development. In fact, in ancient times the letters of the alphabet were used as numbers, that is, by the Greeks and Romans.

Such usage spread to the Arabic language, where the first nine letters came to represent the nine single numbers, with the tenth letter up to the eighteenth representing the decimals, and the nineteenth letter up to the twenty-eighth representing the hundreds. In this way the last letter of the alphabet came to correspond to the number thousand. This is why we said earlier that the Arabic language is the most perfect language, namely, because of the spiritual significance of the number "thousand." The Qur'an says, "A day with your Lord is like a thousand years according to your reckoning." (22:47) It also says: "We have brought it down in the night of Decree. What do you know of the night of Decree? The night of Decree is better than a thousand months" (97:1–3), meaning a thousand years. The Qur'an also provides: "[It is] from God, Lord of [great] ascents. The angels and the Spirit ascend to Him in a day that is equal to fifty thousand years." (70:3–4)

The whole of the Qur'an is pyramidal in structure, with a base and a peak, and its meanings vary from the base to the peak, becoming more and more refined. At the peak the alphabetical letters are used as openings to some chapters. These letters, in turn, are also pyramidal, varying from a base to a peak.

6. This is the classical order of the Arabic alphabet, which is somewhat different from the order used in modern teaching curriculum in schools, although the letters themselves remain the same under both arrangements of their order.

Letters are of three classes: alphabetical letters, vocal letters, and intellectual letters. The alphabetical letters are the known twenty-eight letters, constituting apparent speech. Vocal letters are infinite, including what is audible as well as what is not perceivable by the senses, constituting the thoughts of the conscious. As to the intellectual letters, they are superior to everything else, being the words of God of which He said: "Say, if every sea became ink for the words of my Lord, surely, the sea would be exhausted before the words of my Lord were exhausted, even if a similar amount is brought as additional supply." (18:109) These intellectual letters constitute the thoughts latent in the subconscious mind, at the heart of which lies the eternal truth, with religion on its fringes. Alphabetical, vocal, and intellectual letters are referred to in the verse: "Whether or not you speak aloud, He knows not only what is secret (*sir*), but also what is even more subtle and hidden than that." (20:7) Loud speech corresponds to alphabetical letters; *al-sir*; the secret, corresponds to the vocal letters; while the intellectual letters correspond to *sir al-sir* (secret of the conscience), expressed in the phrase "what is even more subtle than that."[7] Some of these intellectual letters are not perceivable except by the seventh sense.[8]

Reference to these three levels is also made in the verse "Voices faded in reverence for the Gracious [God], so that you can only hear subdued murmur" (20:108), which refers to the audible and the inaudible, in other words, speech through the tongue and speech through thoughts. As to the *sir al-sir* (secret of the conscience), it is expressed in the verse, "All shall submit to the living and all-sustaining God. And he indeed has failed who holds iniquity." (20:111) Iniquity here means subtle polytheism, which is mental repression, which divides the human personality into conflicting and inconsistent conscious and subconscious.

We have already discussed repression in this book and said that it is caused by fear, and that absolute individual freedom requires freedom from fear. To achieve such freedom from any form or type of fear, it is necessary to organize the community in such a way as to secure the individual against fear of the lack of means of subsistence, oppressive authority, and intolerant public opinion. In order to avoid fear, the individual must also have a comprehensive conception of his relationship to the environment and to the essence of that environment. Only thus will the human mind be liberated from inherited fears which still persist in the subconscious.

7. On this see page 71.
8. See pages 94–95 on the sixth and seventh senses.

We have also discussed the Qur'an's reversed or inverted approach, followed by an outward progressive stage, in teaching the human being in accordance with the verse: "We shall show them Our signs in the material world and within themselves, until it becomes manifest to them that He is the Truth. . . . Is your Lord not sufficient witness upon everything?" (41:53) We said earlier that this means that the diligent worshiper endeavors to abandon offensive action, while perhaps still allowing some offensive speech, in a gradual process of improvement. The next step is to abandon offensive speech, while some evil thoughts may be tolerated at the level of the conscious mind. Aggressive thoughts must then be curbed in the conscious mind, until the purification of thought of the subconscious mind is achieved. At this point there is wholesomeness of the heart, and the ability to see in the clarity of the self the Almighty God. From that point begins the outward progressive approach in education. The diligent worshiper at this stage shall be at peace with himself, with his Lord, and with living beings and things. This is Islam at the peak to which God exhorted al-muminin [believers] when He said: "O believers, come into peace (silm) all of you, and follow not the footsteps of Satan; surely, he is your open enemy." (2:208) In this context, "peace" is Islam at its peak.

NATION OF MU'MININ

We have said that the Qur'an was divided between al-iman and al-islam, as well as being revealed in two parts as Meccan and Medinese. The Meccan Qur'an was revealed first. In other words, people were invited to adopt Islam [in the ultimate sense] first, and when they failed to do so, and it was practically demonstrated that they were below its standard, they were addressed in accordance with their abilities. This offer of the higher standard is the conclusive argument against people referred to in the verse: "And We will surely try you until We make manifest those among you who strive [for the cause of God] and those who are steadfast. And We will make known the truth about you." (47:31) This experiment and consequent practical experience is for the benefit of mankind because God's knowledge does not occur afresh (hadith).9 The phrase "those who

9. God in His comprehensive and all-preceding knowledge already knew that Islam would be rejected when first offered in Mecca, but He conducted the experiment for our sake, so that we should know with certainty. God's knowledge is ancient and external beyond time, qadim and not hadith.

strive" means major *jihad*, namely striving to control the self.[10] "And those who are steadfast" refers to endurance of the state of distance from God. "And We will make known the truth about you" means to extract thoughts that are repressed in your subconscious—your *sir al-sir*.

The verses which demonstrate descent from ultimate Islam to the level of *al-iman* are numerous—for example, the verse, "O believers (*mu'minin*), fear God as He ought to be feared, and become true submitters (*muslimin*) before you die." (3:102) When the believers (*mu'minin*) said "which of us can fear God as He ought to be feared?" the Qur'an descended in another verse to the level of "Fear God as much as you can, listen and obey and pay alms, as that is good for yourselves, and those who are rid of their own selfishness are the truly successful ones." (64:16)

When the verse "Those who believe without obscuring their belief with unfairness have security, and they are truly guided" (6:82) was revealed, people found it too difficult to comply with, and they said: "O Messenger of God, which one of us is not unfair to himself?" He replied: "It is not what you mean. Did you not hear what God's true slave (Luqman) said: O son, do not disbelieve in God, such disbelief is great unfairness. The verse means disbelief." The believers were relieved because they knew that they had not disbelieved since the time they came to believe. In fact the Prophet explained the verse to them at the level of *al-mu'minin*, knowing that its explanation at the level of the *al-muslimin* was above their ability, because "unfairness" then means subtle polytheism in the sense mentioned in the verse of the *sir al-sir*. "All shall submit to the living and all-sustaining God. And he indeed has failed who holds iniquity." (20:111)

It is reported about the verse "Those who believe without obscuring their belief with unfairness have security, and they are truly guided" that the Prophet said: "I was told that I am one of them." The Prophet is not merely one of the believers (*al-mu'minin*), as he is the first of the true submitters to God (*al-muslimin*): "Say: 'My prayer and my worship and my life and my death are [all] for God the Lord of all creation. He has no partner. And so am I commanded, and I am the first of those who submit (*al-muslimin*).'" (6:163)

We have said that the nation of the First Message are *al-muslimin*. While the Qur'an described *al-muslimin* at the time of Moses as the Jews, and at the time of Jesus as Christians, it describes them at the time of the First Mohamedan Message as *al-mu'minin* or "those who believed." Listen

10. Reference here is to the Hadith where the Prophet describes self-control as the primary and major *jihad* or self-exertion.

to the Qur'an: "Surely, those who believe and the Jews and the Christians and the Sabians—who so believe in God and the Last Day, and do good deeds—shall have their reward with their Lord, and no fear [shall come] upon them, nor shall they grieve." (2:62) Again, it says "Surely, those who have believed, and the Jews, and the Sabians, and the Christians— who so believe in God and the Last Day and do good deeds—on them [shall come] no fear, nor shall they grieve." (5:69) Another instructive verse reads: "O believers (mu'minin), believe in God, His Messenger, and the Book that He revealed to His Messenger, and the Book revealed previously. He who disbelieves in God, His angels, books, messengers, and the Final Day, has grossly strayed from the path." (4:136) So He calls them mu'minin (believers) and yet invites them to further belief, more iman.

The verses: "O believers (mu'minin), fear God as He ought to be feared, and become true submitters (muslminin) before you die," and "Fear God as much as you can, and listen and obey and pay alms, as that is good for yourselves, and those who are rid of their own selfishness are the truly successful ones" clearly have two different meanings—one setting an original precept and the other a subsidiary one. It is also clear that the real objective is the achievement of the original precept. When it was shown that it was impracticable to do so, it was postponed and the intermediate objective of implementing the subsidiary precept was sought. When the conditions necessary for achieving the original objective, that is to say, when both individual as well as collective human capacities are sufficiently mature, the original precept shall be restored. This is the reason why the original precepts of religion were postponed, and the subsidiary precepts were implemented [as transitional measures] as shall be explained below.

JIHAD IS NOT AN ORIGINAL PRECEPT IN ISLAM

Islam's original view is that a person is free until it is shown, in practice, that he or she is unable to properly discharge the duty of such freedom. Freedom is a natural right corresponding to a duty, namely, its proper exercise. Once a free person is unable to fulfill the duty of his or her freedom, such freedom shall be withdrawn under a law which is consistent with the constitution, that is, a law which reconciles the need of the individual for absolute individual freedom, and the need of the community for total social justice. As already stated, this is the law of *al-mu'awadah* (reciprocity).

This was Islam's original and fundamental principle. The propagation of Islam began with the verses of persuasion in Mecca where the verse "Propagate the path of your Lord in wisdom and peaceable advice, and argue with them in a kind manner. Your Lord is more knowledgeable of those who stray from His path, and He is more knowledgeable of the guided ones" (16:125) and many other similar verses were revealed. This approach was continued for thirteen years, during which time much of the miraculous Qur'an was revealed, and many men, women, and children were transformed under the guidance of the new discipline. The early Muslims curtailed their own aggression against the unbelievers, endured hurt, sacrificed their comforts sincerely and self-denyingly in the cause of spreading their religion, without weakening or submitting. Their lives were the supreme expression of their religion and consisted of sincere worship, kindness, and peaceful coexistence with all other people.

God says: "I have created *jinn* (spirits) and people for no reason except that they may worship Me." (51:56) And He favored people with the mind, body, and comforts that enable them to worship Him and appreciate His Grace. He also says: "God enjoins *al-adl*, justice, *al-ihsan*, the doing of good to others, and benevolence to the next of kin, and forbids indecency, lewdness, manifest evil, and transgression. He admonishes you that you may take heed." (16:90) Again, God says "and that you slay not your children for fear of poverty—it is We who provide for you and for them—and that you approach not foul deeds, whether open or secret; and that you slay not the self, which God has forbidden save in accordance [with the demands of] justice. That is what He has enjoined upon you, that you may understand." (6:151) All this the Qur'an produced in the new religion, and the Prophet and his Companions delivered by their words and example, all to the best interest and advantage of their people.

Nevertheless, their people persisted in worshiping the stone they carved, severing relations with the next of kin, destroying life, and burying girls alive,[11] thereby abusing their freedom, and rendering it liable to be withdrawn. Since at that time there was no law except the sword, the sword was used to that effect [abridging freedom]. Thus,

11. In pre-Islamic days, the Arabs used to bury their daughters alive to avoid any shame they might cause to them, if taken by their enemies, and to avoid having to defend and feed them generally.

implementation shifted from the verse, "Then remind them, as you are only a reminder. You have no dominion over them" (8:21–22) to the verse "except he who shuns and disbelieves, on whom God shall inflict the greatest suffering." (88:23–24). It is as if God said, "We have granted you, Mohamed, dominion over anyone who shuns and disbelieves, so that God shall subject him to minor suffering at your hands through fighting, then God shall also subject him to the greatest suffering in hell." "It is to Us that they shall return. Then We shall hold them to account." (88:25–26) Thus the two first verses were abrogated or repealed by the two second verses. In this way, all the verses of persuasion, though they constitute the primary or original principle, were abrogated or repealed by the verses of compulsion (jihad). This exception was necessitated by the circumstances of the time and the inadequacy of the human capability to discharge properly the duty of freedom at that time. Hence the Prophet said: "I have been instructed to fight people until they declare that la ilah ila-Allah, and that Mohamed is the Messenger of God (etc.). Once they do, they will have secured their lives and property, unless they violate the law. And I leave their sincerity to be judged by God."

Some Muslim scholars believe that Islamic wars were purely defensive wars, a mistaken belief prompted by their keenness to refute claims by the Orientalists that Islam spread by means of the sword. In fact, the sword was used to curtail the abuse of freedom.

Islam used persuasion for thirteen years in propagating its clearly valid message for the individual and the community. When the addressees failed to discharge properly the duties of their freedom, they lost this freedom, and the Prophet was appointed as their guardian until they came of age. However, once they embraced the new religion and observed the sanctity of life and property, and the social claims of their kith and kin, as they had been instructed, the sword was suspended, and abuses of freedom were penalized according to new laws. Hence the development of Islamic Shari'a law, and the establishment of a new type of government.

In justifying the use of the sword, we may describe it as a surgeon's lancet and not a butcher's knife. When used with sufficient wisdom, mercy, and knowledge, it uplifted the individual and purified society. God said to this effect: "We have sent Our Messengers with the clear signs, and revealed with them the Book and the scales, so that people should maintain the fair balance, and decreed iron with much hardship and benefits to people, so that God may discover who supports Him and His Messengers sincerely. God is All-Powerful and Self-Sufficient." (57:25) "We have sent Our Messengers with the clear signs" indicates the conclusive proof of the validity of their messages, "and revealed with them the Book" refers to the principle that la ilah ila-Allah. "The scales" means the Shari'a to adjudicate between slave [man] and the Lord on the one hand, and between one slave and another on the other hand, "so that people should maintain the fair balance" that is to say, be fair in their dealings.

The part "and decreed iron with much hardship and benefits to people" signifies that We have enacted fighting with the sword in order to curtail the freedom of those who abuse it, so that the sword brings them to their senses, thereby allowing them to earn their freedom and benefit from their life. That is, of course, besides other benefits which may be derived from iron, which we need not enumerate here. The part "so that God may discover who supports Him and His Messengers sincerely" is to discover out of practical experience for man's own benefit, because fighting is hateful and difficult. In other words, the object was to see who would endure the hardship of war for the sake of God and in support of the oppressed, by maintaining the fair balance between each individual and himself, and between himself and others. "God is All-Powerful and Self-Sufficient" implies that He is so powerful that He needs no support from anyone else, and nothing can be gained from Him except through His own Grace.

What can be gained from Him in this context is victory. So the verse refers in a subtle way to another verse: "O believers, if you support [the cause of] God, He will help you and will make your steps firm." (47:7) So if you support the cause of God by supporting His Prophet in order to maintain the balance, God shall help you and give you victory over your own lower selves.[12] In other words, if you stand by the cause of God in minor jihad (fighting), He shall support you and give you victory in the major jihad (self-control) where one is helpless without God's help, and no one can give you victory except Him. To "make your steps firm" means tranquility and peace of mind, and includes, of course, physical courage in battle.

In treating ailments of the heart it is wise to begin with gentle means, and to resort to strict measures only when absolutely necessary, deferring drastic treatment to the very end. Suffering death by the sword in this life is really an aspect of suffering hell in the next life, since both are punishments for disbelief. Whoever adds to his own disbelief by inciting

12. On the superior and lower self, ignorant and intelligent selfishness, see the beginning of chapter 3.

others to disbelief or to shun the path of God must be suppressed before he takes up arms in the cause of disbelief. God says: "Those who spend their money in order to shun the path of God shall spend it, achieve only sorrow, and still be defeated. The infidels shall be gathered in hell, so that God may distinguish the bad from the good and set the bad apart and cast them all in hell. These indeed are the losers. Tell the infidels that if they repent, they shall be forgiven for what they have done, but if they persist, then they shall be dealt with as were similar people before them. Fight them to prevent chaos, and so that all religion is rendered unto God; if they give up, then God has insight in what they do." (8:36–39)

When we consider God's expression, "the infidels shall be gathered in hell, so that God may distinguish the bad from the good," we can readily appreciate that the cause of suffering is disbelief. "God has no need for your suffering if you are thankful and believing, God is all-thankful and all-knowledgeable." (4:147) The part of the above text, "Fight them to prevent chaos" means so that there will be no disbelief, its propagation, or the shunning of the path of faith. "[S]o that all religion is rendered unto God" reflects the original purpose of fighting: "Your Lord commanded [that you] worship none but Him." (17:23) This is the design which He shall accomplish regardless of the wishes of the infidels.

In another verse God says: "Fight them to prevent chaos, and in order to render religion unto God; if they desist, then there can be no hostility except against the wrongdoers." (2:193) The wrongdoers are of two levels. On one level there are those who worship other than God, and persist in doing so, while on the other level there are those who appear to submit to God in obedience, but transgress upon the rights of other people and do them injustice. The verse decrees that freedom be withdrawn from those who abuse it, such withdrawal being proportionate to the degree of abuse: for the disbelievers the law of war, and hardship of iron, while to the transgressors, the law of peace and adjudication of rights. This is the meaning of the expression "then there can be no hostility except against the wrongdoers."

Postponement from the original principles to the subsidiary principles signifies descent from the level of al-islam to the level of al-iman. This is referred to in the verse "And We have revealed to you the Reminder [the Qur'an] so that you may explain to mankind that which has been sent down to them, and that they may reflect." (16:44) The phrase "we have revealed to you the Reminder" means the whole of the Qur'an including the original principle—al-islam—as well as the subsidiary (al'iman). "So that you may explain to mankind that which has been sent down to them" means to detail through legislation, and to explain, in various other ways, to the believers (al-mu'minim) what has been brought down to their level. "[T]hat they may reflect," means that perhaps such reflection, while implementing the subsidiary principle, may lead them to the original principle they were unable to implement at the beginning. Here is a subtle reference to the ascent up the various levels of Islam, starting with initial Islam, and ascending by means of clear thinking, guided speech, and sincere action: "Unto Him ascends the pure words, being elevated by good deeds." (35:10)

Thus we reach an extremely important conclusion: many aspects of the present Islamic Shari'a are not the original principles or objectives of Islam. They merely reflect a descent in accordance with the circumstances of the time and the limitations of human ability.

SLAVERY IS NOT AN ORIGINAL PRECEPT IN ISLAM

Islam's original principle is freedom. But the Islamic religion was revealed to a society in which slavery was an integral part of the socioeconomic order. It was also a society that was shown in practice to be incapable of properly exercising its freedom, and therefore its individual members needed guidance; hence the consequent enactment of jihad. In Islamic jihad, the Muslims first had to offer to the unbelievers the new religion. If they refused to accept it, they had the second option of paying jizyah[13] and living under Muslim government, while practicing their own religion and enjoying personal security. If they also refused the option of jizyah, the Muslims would fight them and if victorious take some of them as slaves, thereby adding to the number of those already in slavery.

The rationale of such servitude is to be found in the principle of reciprocity (al-mu'awadah). If an individual is invited to become the slave of God but refuses, such refusal is symptomatic of ignorance that calls for a period of training. The individual prepares to submit voluntarily to the servitude of God by becoming the slave of another person, thereby learning obedience and humility, which are becoming of a slave. Reciprocity (al-mu'awadah) here rules that if a free person refuses to become the slave of God, he may be subjugated and made the slave of a slave of God, in fair and just retribution: "And whoso does an atom's weight of evil will also see it." (99:8)

13. Jizyah is a personal poll tax taken from dhimmis, mainly Jews and Christians living under Muslim rule.

In this way, circumstances and human capacities of the times necessitated propagation of Islam via methods including enslavement, a custom inherited from the more primitive pre-Islamic era. It was neither possible, nor desirable, at that point, for the law to abolish slavery by a stroke of the pen. The needs of the enslaved individuals, as well as the social and economic needs of the community, necessitated the maintenance of the system, while developing it continuously, until every enslaved person would be emancipated. Such period of development is a transitional period during which the slave learns to stand on his own, and earn his honest living within a community that had [also] learned, during the same transitional period, to dispense with the awful exploitation of the slaves in ways that abused their dignity and suppressed their human integrity, as had been their miserable lot during the pre-Islamic period of ignorance.

Islam, in fact, enacted strict regulations for slavery, specifying rights as well as duties for slaves who previously had duties and no rights. Atonement for many sins was granted in exchange for the emancipation of healthy and believing slaves. Islam also enforced any agreements betwen slave and master whereby the slave achieved emancipation after fulfilling certain agreed conditions, thereby achieving full citizenship. Islamic law, moreover, prescribed proper treatment for all slaves. The Prophet said: "Your slaves are your brethren whom God subjected to you, so feed them of your own food, and clothe them of the same material from which you clothe yourselves."

CAPITALISM IS NOT AN ORIGINAL PRECEPT IN ISLAM

Islam's original principle is the common or joint possession of property amongst the slaves of God, so that each one takes according to his needs, the basic needs of a traveler [passing through this life to the next true and lasting life]. This principle was adhered to, in an exemplary way, by the only true Muslim of the time, the Prophet. Islam, however, came to a people with no experience of this principle of sharing, understanding only the concept of private property. No government had made claims on their property, and they found it difficult even to pay zakah from their "own" property. The reluctance was the reason for their apostasy from Islam when the Prophet passed away.14 It is with respect to such people that God says:

14. The reference here is to some Muslims who repudiated their faith and refused to pay zakah upon the Prophet's death. Abu Bakr, the first Khalifa, or successor of the Prophet, had

This life is merely play, and amusement. If you believe and fear God, He shall reward you, and not ask you for your property. If He asked you for your property, that would expose you, as you would refuse and display your grudge and malice. Here you are being invited to spend property in the cause of God, and some of you fail to do so. He who fails to spend is withholding himself. God is Rich; it is you who are poor. If you fail, God shall replace you with other people who shall not be like you. (47:37–39)

The phrase "This life is merely play and amusement" means that it is a period of heedlessness, ignorance, and childish irresponsibility. "If you believe" in God and His Messenger, "and fear Him," by avoiding disbelief, polytheism, and major sins, "He shall reward you" for such good deeds. The phrase "[He shall] not ask you for your property" means He shall not ask you to give up everything as alms. "If He asked you for your property, that would expose you as you would refuse," means that if He asked you to give up everything, you would fail to comply with such a difficult order, "and display your grudge and malice" or express your hidden love for property, weakness of faith, and dormant polytheism. "If you fail, God shall replace you with other people who shall not be like you" is a subtle reference to the coming of the superior true submitters to God (al-muslimin) following al-mu'minin. This is the reason why current Islamic legislation regarding property does not reflect Islam's real objective, but gradually introduces Muslims, without undue hardship, to the true Islamic concept of property. Thus, zakah was introduced and made one of the pillars of the faith, through the grace of God.15

INEQUALITY BETWEEN MEN AND WOMEN IS NOT AN ORIGINAL PRECEPT IN ISLAM

Islam's original precept is complete equality between men and women, as indicated by their equal responsibility before God in the Day of Judgment, when the scales of deeds are set. God says: "Nor does any bearer of burden bear the burden of another, no matter how overburdened, and not even of a kin. You are to warn [those] who sincerely fear God and perform the prayer. And he who pays alms (zakah) is cleansing

---

to fight and force them back into the community through what is known as hurwb al-ridah, the apostasy wars.

15. In other words, God allowed Muslims to maintain private ownership of property and demanded payment of zakah, a minute proportion, as a stage in preparing them for socialism as will be explained in the next chapter.

himself, and to God [you] shall all return." (6:164) He also says: "Today each soul is rewarded for what it earned, without unfairness. Surely God is swift at reckoning." (40:17) God also says: "Every soul is pledged for what it has earned." (74:38)

But Islam was revealed at a time and to a people who went so far as to bury girls alive in fear of the disgrace if they were taken as spoils of war, or to avoid the burden of having to feed them in time of drought and famine. God describes the phenomenon: "When one is told that he has had a daughter born, his face darkens with suppressed grief. He hides himself from the people because of the bad news he has had. Shall he keep it in spite of disgrace or shall he bury it in the dust? Verily, evil is that which they judge." (16:58–59) Thus, neither society as a whole, nor women in particular, were ready for the ultimate good Islam had for women. A transitional period was necessary for both men and women individually, as well as for society as a whole to develop. Hence, the law gave women half what men had in inheritance and testimonial competence. Women had to submit to men as fathers, brothers, and husbands: "Men are guardians over women because of the advantage they have over women and because [men] spend [on women] of their wealth." (4:34) Early Islamic legislation was, in fact, a great leap forward for women, in comparison to their previous status. Nevertheless, it was far below Islam's ultimate objective.

POLYGAMY IS NOT AN ORIGINAL PRECEPT IN ISLAM

Islam's original precept is marriage between one man and one woman, without dowry or divorce. Prohibition of polygamy is implied in the verse "and if you fear you will not be able to do justice [among your wives] then [marry only] one" (4:3), when read with the verse, "And you cannot maintain [perfect] balance between wives, however much you may desire it." (4:129) Prohibition of divorce is also suggested in the Hadith: "The most hateful permissible thing to God is divorce." The subtle implication being that since God hates divorce, He is bound to prohibit it when that is possible and practicable. God always achieves what He wants.

Islam's rejection, on principle, of the concept of dowry was based on the fact that the dowry represents the price of a woman at a time in history when women were taken in one of three ways: as spoils of war, by kidnapping, or by purchasing them. As such, the dowry is a mark of women's inherited insignificance that must be discontinued when women's dignity and integrity are realized through the implementation of Islam's original precept. Prior to Islam women were granted virtually no dignity or respect. Marital relationships were not based on human consideration and kindness. A man would marry as many as ten or twenty women to bear his children and work for him.

Another feature of pre-Islamic society was the fact that the number of women exceeded the number of men, since many men perished in wars. So Islam limited polygamy, but did not immediately impose monogamy, since under that system a great many women would have remained unprotected and unprovided for spinsters. Early Islam limited a man to four wives, as God says: "Marry of women as many as may be agreeable to you, two or three or four; and if you fear you will not be able to do justice [among your wives] then [marry only] one." (4:3) Then comes a subtle hint of the difficulty of maintaining fairness between wives in the verse: "And you cannot maintain [perfect] balance between wives, however much you may desire it. But incline not wholly [to one] so that you leave [the other] like [a thing] suspended. And if you are reconciled and act righteously, surely God is Most Forgiving [and] Merciful." (4:129) Thus it [Shari'a, or early Islamic legislation] descended from "perfect" justice which is required in the original religious principle, because that was premature for society as well as individual men and women. Instead, relative justice was accepted in Shari'a. The phrase "And you cannot maintain [perfect] balance between wives, however much you may desire it" continued to add: "But incline not wholly [to one] so that you leave [the other] like [a thing] suspended." In this way, the required balance was restricted to material things and did not include emotional attachment. That leniency made polygamy possible and bearable, since it was unavoidable at that stage in [mu'minin] society.

Justice in this context is limited in the same way freedom may be limited: that is, as a right, it has a corresponding duty, and anyone failing to recognize the duty is denied the right. Women at that time were too backward to be equal to men. Thus, relative justice was beneficial both for women and for society at the time. Polygamy, however, was a transitional stage leading to eventual complete equality between men and women, at which point "balance" and justice would include emotional attachment as well. In this way, the precondition of "if you fear you will not be able to do justice [among your wives]" operates to prohibit polygamy, except under certain contingencies, specified by law, and subject to the consent of the aggrieved party [the wife].

DIVORCE IS NOT AN ORIGINAL PRECEPT IN ISLAM

Islam's original precept is the continuity of the relationship between spouses. Thus, a man's wife is his corresponding part, the manifestation of his self outside himself. She is the totality of outward signs corresponding to the man's self in terms of the verse: "We shall show them Our signs in the material world, and within themselves, until it becomes manifest to them that He is the Truth. Is your Lord not sufficient witness upon everything?" (41:53) But we lack the insight to select our second half correctly. We are like a blind person who sits with pegs in his hands, some of which are square, others rectangular, triangular, circular, semicircular, and in other sectors of a circle, and with a surface in front of him, on which there are holes, each corresponding to one of the pegs he holds in his hands. He attempts to fit the right peg into the right hole, and succeeds once while failing to do so several times. He may even fail to fit the peg in any hole altogether. In fact, this example does not quite describe our efforts to select a spouse. A blind person in the above example is better off, and more likely to succeed, than anyone of us trying to make this choice. So, when one misses by placing a circular peg into a square hole, for example, he needs a second chance to repeat the experiment all over again. Divorce is permitted in order to give us such a second chance.

When Adam and Eve fell through sin and were expelled from paradise, they descended to earth separated, and began to look for each other: Adam looking for Eve, and Eve looking for Adam. After much search, Adam found Eve without really finding her, and Eve found Adam, without really finding him. From that day to the present, each Adam is looking for his Eve, and each Eve is looking for her Adam. The doors of misguidance are wide open, while the doors of guidance are narrow. But thanks to God, we are receiving more light every day through which the circle of misguidance is receding, while the circle of guidance is widening. The light of faith is not enough, and it was not enough for al-mu'minin to make the right choice. Once God completes His light and the sun of Islam arises, then there will be no mistake in the choice that needs correction through divorce, as counterparts meet and complete union is achieved, "every people shall know their drinking place." (7:160)

Marriage in Islam is an eternal relationship. Legal marriage under Shari'a is an attempt by which a man and a woman seek to achieve the relationship which used to exist between Adam and Eve, when Eve was taken out of Adam: "O people, fear your Lord Who created you from a single Self and of it [too] He created a mate, and from the twain spread many men and women; and fear God, in Whose Name you appeal to one another, and [fear Him particularly respecting] ties of kinship. Verily, God watches over you." (4:1) Divorce recognizes man's tendency to err and learn from his mistakes. The Shari'a rule allowing divorce will be ultimately abrogated when there is no longer any need for it.

THE VEIL (AL-HIJAB) IS NOT AN ORIGINAL PRECEPT IN ISLAM

Islam's original precept is *al-sufur*. [16] The purpose of Islam is chastity, emanating from within men and women, and not imposed through closed doors and long robes. There is no way to achieve inner chastity, however, except through education and discipline, and this requires a transitional period when chastity is encouraged through the veil, hence the rule imposing it. The original precept is that which prevailed between Adam and Eve before they committed their first sin:

> O Adam, live with your wife in Paradise, eat whatever you wish, but do not approach this tree, lest you become wrongdoers. The devil whispered to them in order to reveal to them what had been concealed from them of their private parts, so he said: Your Lord forbade you this tree in order to prevent you from becoming angels or immortal. He swore to them that he was giving them good advice. He thereby misled them in vanity, and once they tasted the tree, they discovered their private parts and started to cover them with leaves from Paradise. Their Lord called them: Did I not forbid you from approaching that tree, and warn you that the devil is your enemy? They said: Our Lord, we have wronged ourselves, if Thou forgive us not, and have not mercy on us, we shall surely be of the lost. He said: Descend, some of you shall be enemies for each other, and you shall settle and enjoy life on earth for awhile. He said: On it you shall live, and die, and out of it you shall come. O children of Adam, we have given you clothing and feathers to cover your private parts, but chastity emanating from the fear of God is better, all this is of the signs of God that they may remember. O children of Adam, do not allow the devil to lead you stray as he expelled your parents from Paradise, stripping them in order to show them their private parts; he

16. *Al-hijab* as required by Shari'a is the covering of all of the woman's body except her face and hands. *Al-sufur*, on the other hand, permits more exposure, provided modest and decent dress is maintained in general.

and his tribe can see you, while you cannot see them. We have made the devils friends for those who do not believe. (7:19–27)

The phrase "in order to reveal to them" means to show them "what has been concealed from them," through clothing of light,[17] "of their private parts." The phrase "he thereby misled them in vanity" means he advised them in falsehood until they committed sin. Once they fell, "they discovered their private parts, and started to cover them with leaves from Paradise," that is, they began to cover their private parts with fig leaves. From that day began the veil (al-hijab). It is therefore the consequence of sin, and shall accompany it until they vanish together, God willing. The verse, "O children of Adam, we have given you clothing and feathers to cover your private parts" signifies that We have created for you, and imposed upon you, the weaving of cotton, wool, and other material to cover your private parts. The phrase "chastity from fear of God is better" implies the clothing of true belief (tawhid), chastity, and modesty implanted into your hearts is better than clothing of cotton. But "all this is of the signs of God" means that cotton clothing is one of the signs of God and His wisdom of legislation "so that they may remember" the state of cleanliness, innocence, and chastity they had, before committing sin, and return to it. The last verse clearly demonstrates our argument with respect to al-hijab.

Al-sufur is an original principle in Islam, because it is consistent with the original principle of freedom. As stated above, the original principle in Islam is that everyone is free until he or she abuses his freedom, when that freedom is withdrawn according to a law that is consistent with the constitution, as explained above.

One can see the wisdom of al-hijab in the verse: "And such of your women as are guilty of [any] flagrant impropriety, call to witness four of you against them; and if they bear witness, then confine them to the house until death overtakes them or God opens for them some other way." (4:15) When there is sufficient evidence of misconduct short of adultery, calling for the penalty (hadd) of fornication, then a woman's freedom is withdrawn by denying her al-sufur; and she is held at home until she dies, unless she has clearly benefitted from her confinement and begins to behave well, that is, would no longer abuse her freedom of al-sufur.

Al-hijab is therefore a rational penalty for the abuse of freedom of al-sufur. This is the original principle in Islam. Al-hijab, as practiced at

17. That is to say, unawareness due to fundamental and original innocence.

present, is a continuing abrogation of the freedom of *al-sufur*, designed by Shari'a to be a safeguard for the immature believers *(al-mu'minin)*. Only true submitters *(al-muslimin)* can shoulder the responsibility of *al-sufur*, hence they are not subject to *al-hijab*.

SEGREGATION OF MEN FROM WOMEN IS NOT AN ORIGINAL PRECEPT IN ISLAM

What may be said of *al-sufur* applies to desegregation or mixing between men and women. The original precept in Islam is the desegregated community of men and women, which is at the same time free from the permissiveness that afflicts present-day desegregated societies.

These examples demonstrate the divergence between the primary and subsidiary precepts of Islam, and that the First Message lowered the standards of the Second Message, in order to suit the times and serve its society. It [the First Message] takes account of human weaknesses and limited capacities, and was undeniably necessary in early Islam.

6

The Second Message of Islam

The Second Message is Islam. The Prophet himself imparted this Second Message without elaboration or detail, except for such overlaps between the First Message and the Second Message as *'ibadat* and *hudod* [worship practices and the specified penalties]. God says: "Today I have perfected your religion for you, completed My grace upon you, and sanctioned Islam as your religion." (5:3) That day was the day of *'arafah* on *hajat al-wada'* (the farewell pilgrimage) of the eighth year of *hijrah*, which was a Friday. This verse is the last verse of the Qur'an to be revealed, and is the ultimate word of the Divine Message.

God has accepted Islam for mankind so that we may accept it, because anything that is not initiated by Him cannot be undertaken by us. God says: "Then He forgave them in order that they may repent." (9:118)[1]

Many people considered the phrase "Today I have perfected your religion for you" as implying that Islam itself has been fully achieved by mankind on earth on that day. The verse: "And We have revealed to you the Reminder [the Qur'an] so that you may explain to mankind that which has been sent down to them" (16:44) was also taken to mean that the Qur'an has already been finally and conclusively explained. Nothing, however, is further from the truth than this view. "Explanation" of the Qur'an has been only in terms of [expedient] legislation, the Shari'a, and interpretation to the extent appropriate for the time of such explanation

---

1. That is to say, people's repentance is initiated by God before it can be undertaken by them.

and in accordance with the capacity of the audience and the abilities of the people.

The Qur'an can never be finally and conclusively explained. Islam, too, can never be concluded. Progress in it is eternal: "Surely, the [true] religion with God is Islam." (3:19) "With God" [is eternal] beyond time and space. Progress into Islam by means of the Qur'an is progress towards God in infinitude (al-itlaq). As such it has not been, and can never be, fully and conclusively explained. It is its revelation into al-mashaf [Arabic text] as a Book that has been concluded, but its explanation has not.

This is how one should understand the difference between "revealed" and "explain" in the verse "And we have revealed to you the Reminder [the Qur'an] so that you may explain to mankind that which has been sent down to them, and they may reflect." According to the prevailing understanding of Muslim scholars, the two notions are synonymous, while in fact they are not. The level of understanding in the phrase "that which has been sent down to them" does not refer to the whole of the Qur'an but only to the part subject to explanation, namely the First Message, and sections where the First and the Second Messages overlap.

The Qur'an was revealed with dual meanings. God says in this connection: "God has revealed the best speech in a Book of similar and dual meanings, from which the skin of those who fear their Lord creeps! Then their skin and hearts soften to al-dhikr [remembrance through worship of God]. That is the guidance of God with which He guides whomsoever He wishes, and he whom God misguided has no other guide." (30:23) The word "similar" implies that there is some similarity between the Qur'an at its base and at its peak, its front and back. Its zahir and batin, "dual meanings," refer to its two levels of meaning: a distant meaning with the Lord, and a nearer meaning that has come down to the slave [of God].

The whole of the Qur'an is of dual meanings: every verse and word and even every letter has a dual meaning. The reason for this is that the Qur'an is the Lord's speech to His slave. The similarity in the Qur'an is due to the similarity between the Lord and the slave, expressed by the Prophet in the Hadith, "God has created Adam [man] after His Own image." God expresses the same meaning in the verse: "O people, fear your Lord, Who has created you from a single Self." (4:1) That "single Self" means His Own Blessed and Exalted Self.

The word Islam, for example, has a near meaning exposed by the Qur'an in the verse, "The Bedouins said amunna [we believe], tell them you have not believed, but say asslummna [we submit] and al-'iman [true belief] did not enter your hearts yet." (40:14) This is what we termed initial Islam which, we said, is not taken by God as significant. Islam has a further meaning which lies with God in infinity. To this further meaning comes the reference in the verse: "Oh believers [mu'minin], fear God as He ought to be feared and become true submitters [muslimin] before you die." (3:102)

It goes without saying that no one fears God as He ought to be feared except God Himself. This is, therefore, a methodology of ascent to God through many levels of servitude, humility, and submission. Servitude is infinite, just like Lordship. Absolute servitude to God requires absolute knowledge of God, and this only God can achieve. "Say no one knows what is in heaven and earth, the Unknown, except God." (27:65) The Unknown here means God Himself, so it is as if He said, "No one knows God except God Himself." In our book Rasalat al-Salah, which may be consulted in this context, we have shown how servitude [to God] is freedom.

Islam is a method of ascent to servitude, and the Qur'an is the Book which leads the way. This quality of the Qur'an is the reason it was revealed, as indicated in the verse, "And, indeed, We rendered the Qur'an for the sake of al-dhikr, remembrance through worship, is there anyone who would take heed?" (54:17) The Qur'an reminds us of servitude which we have accepted and then forgotten:

> And [remember] when thy Lord brought forth from Adam's children—out of their loins—their offspring and made them bear witness against their own selves saying, "Am I not your Lord?" They said: "Yes, we admit this." [This He did] lest you should say on the Day of Resurrection, "we were surely unaware of this." Or [lest] you should say, [it was] only our fathers [who] associated co-partners [with God] in the past and we were merely a generation after them. Will Thou then destroy us for what those, who lied, did? And thus do We make clear the Signs, [that they may be admonished] and that they may return [to God]. (7:172–74)

So that they may return to God in servitude and submission, through Islam.

As the Qur'an is the methodology of ascent to God, "We said: Go forth hence, all of you. And if there comes to you guidance from Me, then whoso shall follow My guidance, on them [shall come] no fear, nor shall they grieve." (2:38) Since the Qur'an is that guidance, then it has its beginning with God, and its end with us. If we proceed properly through its levels, we shall recover the paradise we lost through the sin of Adam, and ascend into infinity (al-itlaq). God said of the Qur'an: "Alif lam min. That is certainly the Book which contains guidance for the God fearing." (2:1–2) Of those who fear God who are guided by the Qur'an, He said: "Those who fear God are in paradise, and a river, on a seat of truth, with the Most Able King." (54:54) These are levels or grades, beginning with paradise, then the river, then the seat of truth, and finally with the Most Able King in infinity. Such levels vary from physical paradise—which is the paradise lost through sin, to the Absolute in His itlaq. The Qur'an guides to all this, hence it is inexhaustible: "Say, if every sea became ink for the words of my Lord, surely, the sea would be exhausted before the words of my Lord were exhausted, even if a similar amount is brought as additional supply." (18:109) For this reason it is false to assert that the Qur'an may be finally and conclusively explained. The Qur'an is God's dhat [Self or Soul] which has descended, out of pure grace, to levels comprehensible by the slaves, thereby becoming the Qur'an in its various levels of descent: al-dhikr, al-Qur'an, and al-furqan. [2] Al-furqan was the most effective form of Arabic expression to indicate the two levels of al-Qur'an and al-dhikr. The Qur'an was rendered into the form of Arabic expression so that we might understand from God. God says in this respect: "We have rendered it into Arabic so that you may understand." (43:3) This verse and other similar verses have misled many Muslim scholars into believing that the Qur'an itself is Arabic, in the sense that its meanings may be exhaustively understood through the Arabic language. It is not so, as we have explained when discussing Qur'anic chapters starting with letters of the alphabet, above.

Being so supreme, Islam has never been achieved by any nation up to the present day. The nation of muslimin has not yet come. It is expected to come, however, in the future of humanity. Its day of emergence shall be the day of the ultimate pilgrimage, the day when the Divine statement "Today I have perfected your religion for you, completed My grace upon you, and sanctioned Islam as your religion" (5:3) is realized in practice.

Mohamed, in his time, was the pioneer of the muslimin to come. It was as if he came to his nation, the nation of the mu'minin from the future. He was not one of them, as he was the only Muslim amongst them. "Say: My prayer and my worship and my life and my death are [all]

2. These terms refer to the Qur'an at different levels of knowledge and understanding of the truth in its batin, beyond the superficial zahir meaning of the text.

for God the Lord of all creation. He has no partner. And so am I commanded, and I am the first of those who submit [al-muslimin]." (6:163) Abu Bakr, the second best man, was the most superior of all the believers (al-mu'minin), yet there was a huge gap between him and the Prophet. It was to future al-muslimin that the Prophet referred, when he said:

> "How I long for my brothers who have not come yet." And Abu Bakr said: "Are we not your brothers, O Messenger of God?" He replied: "No, you are my Companions!" Then he said again: "How I long for my brothers who have not come yet!" Then Abu Baker said: "Are we not your brothers, O Messenger for God?" He said: "No, you are my companions!" Then He said for the third time: "How I long for my brothers who have not come yet!" They asked: "Who are your brothers, O Messenger of God?" He said: "A people who come at the end of time, of whom the active one shall have seventy times as much reward as you have." They asked: "Seventy times as much as we have or they have?" He replied: "As you have." They asked: "Why?" He replied: "Because you find assistance in doing good, and they find no assistance."

THE MUSLIMS (AL-MUSLIMIN)

The Muslims, as a nation, have not yet come, but the Prophet prophesied their coming, towards the end of time, when circumstances are suitable, and God's promise is fulfilled: "And he who seeks a religion other than Islam, it shall not be accepted of him and in the Hereafter he shall be among the losers." (3:85) On that day all people shall embrace religion and find no alternative, because religion provides the only answers.

We believe that the earth is preparing for the emergence of the Islamic Shari'a of the true submitters (al-muslimin), which shall establish the new civilization. In view of the bankruptcy of contemporary social philosophies, there is no alternative. As stated at the outset of this book, the whole of humanity today is in an ideological wilderness, with Western civilization lost and bankrupt,[3] and with issues of democracy, socialism, and individual freedom persistently demanding answers. Yet there is no answer except through the cross-fertilization of Western civilization, or to be more precise, Western material progress, with a new spirit, namely, the

3. As indicated above, the author includes both the Marxist and liberal traditions when he refers to Western civilization.

spirit of Islam. Islam appears to be the only ideology capable of resolving the existing conflict between the individual and the community and between the individual and the universe, as we have already demonstrated.

We should not confuse the name *Muslims* with the traditional name given to the present nation. We have already stated that the present nation derives its name from the initial Islam. Actually, present Muslim society is the nation of the *al-mu'minin* [believers]. No nation up to now has deserved the name *al-muslimin*. Any mention of Islam with respect to previous nations refers merely to initial Islam, except for the pioneers of humanity who achieved ultimate Islam, or rather a degree of the ultimate Islam, as the ultimate Islam can never be exhaustively achieved. Such pioneers are, therefore, the pioneers of the nation of *al-muslimin* which has not come yet. God says in this connection:

> And [remember the time] when Abraham and Ishmael raised the foundations of the House [praying]: "Our Lord, accept [this] from us for Thou art the All-Hearing, the All-Knowing. Our Lord, make both of us submissive to Thee and make of our offspring a people submissive to Thee. And show us our ways of worship and turn to us with mercy; for Thou art Oft-Returning [with compassion, and art] Merciful. And, Our Lord, raise up among them a Messenger from among themselves, who may recite to them Thy Signs and teach them the Book and Wisdom and may purify them; surely, Thou art the Mighty, the Wise." And who will turn away from the religion of Abraham but he who makes a fool of himself. Him did We choose in this world, and in the next he will surely be among the righteous. When his Lord said to him, "Submit," he said, "I [hereby] submit to the Lord of the worlds." The same did Abraham enjoin upon his sons,—and Jacob [also—saying] "O my sons, truly God has chosen this religion for you; so let not death overtake you except when you are in a state of complete submission" Were you present when death came to Jacob, when he said to his sons, "What will you worship after me?" They answered, "We will worship thy God, the God of thy fathers, Abraham and Ishmael and Isaac, the One God; and to Him we submit ourselves." (2: 127–33)

The phrase "Our Lord, make both of us submissive to Thee" refers to ultimate Islam, and they [Abraham and Ishmael] were in fact *muslimin* [in this sense of ultimate Islam]. But the phrase "and make of our offspring a people submissive to Thee" indicates, in the short run, a Muslim nation in the sense of initial Islam, which shall evolve and develop into the ultimate Islam. Their prayers have been answered. Abraham advised his sons that there is no god except God, *la ilah ila-Allah*, and so did Jacob: "O my sons, truly God has chosen this religion for you; so let not death overtake you except when you are in a state of complete submission"— that is to say, remain holding fast to the creed and maintain that *la ilah ila Allah* until your death. Their answer, "we will worship thy God, the God of thy fathers Abraham and Ishmael and Isaac, the One God; and to Him we submit ourselves," refers to the initial Islam.

God also said: "As I inspired the disciples [of Christ] to believe in Me, and in My Messengers, they said: We do believe, and You shall bear witness that we have submitted *(muslimin).*" (5:111) Their Islam here is synonymous with *al-'iman* [faith], as required in the revelation. God in the revelation required them to believe. When they did believe and declared this, they thought that their *'iman* was Islam, so they said: "You shall bear witness that we have submitted *(muslimin).*" A knowledgeable person can hear the Lord replying: "Do not say we have surrendered, but say we believe." They had not surrendered in the sense of the ultimate Islam. They merely surrendered in the sense of the initial Islam.

The disciples were Muslims in the sense of initial Islam, since even the first stage of ultimate Islam requires moving out of the law for the community as a whole, and entering upon *Shari'a fardiyah*, the law for the individual. Individuality is achieved only after perfect compliance with the law for the community, until one is able to properly exercise his absolute individual freedom. The ultimate Islam is the level of individualities.

Individuality cannot be achieved by anyone who is divided within himself. When the conscious mind is no longer in conflict with the subconscious, unity of being is attained, and this is characterized by wholesomeness of the heart, clarity of thought, and beauty of body, thereby realizing a full and comprehensive intellectual and emotional life. "The next life is the ultimate life if they only know." (29:64) Ultimate life, free from defects, disease and death, indeed the opposite of death.

To restore unity to one's being is for an individual to think as he wishes, speak what he thinks, and act according to his speech. This is the objective of Islam: "O believers, why do you say what you do not do? It is most hateful to God that you say what you do not do." (61:2–3)

THE GOOD SOCIETY

This superior state can only be reached through a two-fold method: first, the good society, and secondly, the scientific educational method to be adopted by the individual in order to liberate himself from inherited fear.

The good society is one that is based on three equalities: economic equality, today known as socialism, or the sharing of wealth; political equality or democracy, or sharing in political decisions which affect daily life; and social equality which, to some extent, results from socialism and democracy, and is characterized by a lack of social classes and discrimination based on color, faith, race, or sex. In the good society, people are judged according to their intellectual and moral character, as reflected in their public and private lives and demonstrated in the spirit of public service at all times and through every means. Social equality aims at removing social classes and differences between urban and rural life by providing equal opportunities for cultural refinement. The criterion of social equality is that marriage [the most fundamental and intimate relation] is possible between any man and any woman. This is the accurate test of social equality.

A good society also enjoys tolerant public opinion, permitting different life-styles and manners, as long as these are beneficial to society.

Public opinion has its own judgments over and above those of the law and may be more effective than legislation itself in deterring deviants and offenders. Public opinion may, of course, condemn any type of conduct it disapproves, but it must always do so only by nonviolent means, since violence usually results in one of two evil responses: counterviolence or hypocrisy. Sometimes public opinion can be enacted as legislation if this is consistent with the constitution as described above [that is, legislation that reconciles the individual need for absolute individual freedom and society's need for complete social justice].

ECONOMIC EQUALITY: SOCIALISM

There is no room here for detailed examination of socialism, and we propose to expand this theme in a book entitled *Islam is Democratic and Socialist.* 4

Socialism means that people share the wealth of the earth. Since society began, socialism developed along with capitalism. Capitalism, or individual ownership, was for a long while the basis of society, and

4. This book, to which the author refers several times in this chapter, was never written and published as such. The author did, however, cover this subject in numerous essays and public lectures, some of which have been published in book form in Arabic.

evolved until it reached its present level. Socialism developed in a similar manner, but at a much slower pace, because capitalism is a natural prelude to socialism. Again, socialism derives from the rule of law that safeguards the rights of the weak, while capitalism derives from the law of the jungle, of the dominance of the strong. Naturally, the law of the jungle precedes the law of justice and compassion.

Socialism, in its most primitive form, began as the envy felt by the "have nots" towards the "haves." Possession of, for example, light, strong, and sharp stone tools or weapons, a spacious and secure cave, or a beautiful, loving, obedient, and healthy wife prompted the historic struggle between the "haves" and the "have nots." This struggle will continue until there is absolute equality between all individuals in sharing of the wealth of the earth.

Before scientific socialism appeared on the scene, primitive socialism already organized a sharing of certain types of common wealth. As it was expressed by the Prophet, "People are partners in three things: water, pasture, and fire." This could be taken as approval, indicating that we should implement socialism in general when goods are abundant through proper exploitation of natural and industrial resources.

Socialism reached its scientific phase only recently, and became so popular with the various peoples of the world that many claim it today, whether they really mean it or not. By the beginning of the nineteenth century, the terms "socialism" and "communism" had made their appearance with respect to public ownership of immoveable property. Robert Owen, a rich industrialist who is generally regarded as the founder of modern socialism, first used the term "socialism" around 1820. Owen believed it was possible to achieve social change through slow and orderly constitutional development, as opposed to the violent horrors of ill-prepared revolution.

The word "communism" is derived from a Latin word meaning "common" or owned by all, and was used for the first time around 1835 by French secret revolutionary committees. These committees aimed to overthrow the middle class by force and establish a new economic order of common ownership and government by the proletariat.

Karl Marx later formulated and developed the various theories and practices of socialism and communism. He preferred the term communism for his system because it was associated with the notion of violent social change. His ideology was based on four principles:

1. The course of history is determined by economic forces.

THE SECOND MESSAGE 155

2. History is nothing but a record of class struggle.
3. Government is only a tool used by one class to suppress the other classes.
4. Violence and force are the only means of achieving any fundamental change in society.

In accordance with these principles, Marx continued to criticize the socialist experiments supervised by Robert Owen. He described them as unscientific and unrealistic because history, in his view, was governed by scientific laws, and no fundamental social change could ever be achieved without the use of force and violence. He scorned Owen's view and those of other socialists that social change could be achieved through comradeship, cooperation, and slow development. He described other socialists' approach as idealistic socialism, while referring to his own system as "scientific" socialism, or "communism."

When we speak of "scientific socialism," we do not mean Marx's approach. In fact, Marx's socialism was not truly scientific because it suffered from a basic error, which we shall deal with in detail in our forthcoming book, *Islam is Democratic and Socialist*, God willing.[5]

Scientific socialism, in our view, is founded on two concurrent principles: first, increased production from such resources as minerals, agriculture, animal wealth, and industry by means of science, technology, and administration; and second, equitable distribution involving the setting of maximum and minimum limits to personal incomes in such a way that the minimum limit is guaranteed to every citizen, including children, old people, and the disabled, at a level sufficient to sustain dignified human existence. The gap between maximum and minimum income must not be wide enough to create a higher class which refuses to marry from the low-income class. In order to increase production, ownership of the means of production must be prohibited to a single individual or a few individuals, whether associating for production or distribution. No citizen should own anything individually except a house and surrounding garden, furniture, a car. The key here is that no one should be allowed to own anything that permits the exploitation of one citizen's labor to increase the income of another. Individual ownership, even within such narrow boundaries, should not be ownership of property

5. The author addressed some of the issues in a public lecture which was later published in a booklet entitled *Al-Marxiyah fi Al-Mizan* ("A Critique of Marxism"), which has not yet been translated.

as such, but rather ownership of the benefits derived from property, and all property remains in the ownership of God and the community as a whole.

As production from resources increases, the equity of distribution is perfected, and differences are reduced by raising both minimum and maximum incomes. But the gap between minimum and maximum incomes is gradually narrowed in order to achieve absolute equality. When such absolute equality is achieved through the grace of God, and as a result of abundant production, we shall achieve communism or a sharing of the earth's wealth by all people. Communism thus differs from socialism in degree, in the sense that socialism is a stage in the development towards communism.

The Prophet experienced ultimate communism, where his own personal law was in accordance with the verse of ultimate *zakah*: "When they ask you what to give away, say all that you do not need" (2:219), meaning all that you do not immediately need. He also spoke of *al-Ash'ariun*,[6] at the level of communism where he said: "When *al-Ash'ariun* had difficult times, or were traveling, they would spread a piece of cloth, place all the food they had on it, and share it amongst themselves in equal shares. Those are people to whom I belong, and they belong to me." This is the concept of the nation of *muslimin* that is yet to come. The *sufis* appreciated this, so they imagined the whole earth, with all its wealth, as a table brought down by God to His creation, telling each of them to carry the supplies of a traveler, and continue the journey towards Him. The earth is like a laid table, with meat, bread, vegetables, sweets, with ten people sitting around it. Everything on the table belongs to all of them, and no one owns a piece of meat, for example, until he holds it with his fingers and takes it into his mouth.

When the Qur'an tells us of paradise, it says: "And they say: 'All praise belongs to God Who has made good to us His promise, and has given us the earth to inherit, we shall make our abode in the Garden wherever we please.' How excellent is the reward of the [righteous] workers." (39:74) This is, in fact, a model of the ultimate paradise to be realized on earth when, as the Prophet said, "Justice shall fill the earth in the same way it was previously full of injustice." This is what Marx dreamed of, but failed to find the way to achieve. It can only be achieved by *al-muslimin* who are yet to come, and then the earth shall enjoy a

6. A tribe in southern Arabia.

degree of fulfillment of the verse: "The God-fearing are in gardens and springs. They will be told: Enter therein, in peace and security. We cleansed what was in their breasts of hatred, so they became brothers sitting together, never to feel hardship or be removed therefrom." (15:45–48) This is the degree of communism to be achieved by Islam with the coming of the nation of *muslimin*, whence the earth shall light up with the Light of its Lord, and God's Grace is conferred upon its inhabitants, when there shall be peace, and love shall triumph.

POLITICAL EQUALITY: DEMOCRACY

Again, we will not discuss democracy in detail here, as it will be discussed in our book *Islam is Democratic and Socialist*. Just as socialism is the product of the struggle between the "haves" and the "have nots" in the material sphere, democracy is the product of the struggle between those same extremes in the political sphere. Its purpose is the sharing of power. Democracy parallels socialism; they are as two wings of society. In the same way that a bird does not fly with one wing, so does society need the two wings of democracy and socialism.

Socialism, which requires greater social awareness, is preceded by democracy which, in the beginning, may be exercised by only a few enlightened individuals. Scientific socialism also needs, as a base, the riches of developed capitalism as well as the advances of modern technology. Primitive, native socialism, however, has its origins in ancient history.

Democracy was born in Athens, the most culturally advanced of the Greek city-states. Each of those cities had its own independent government. As the city-states were small, it was easy for the entire population to participate in government through public assemblies. Greek democracy was, therefore, direct democracy, with no need for an elected house of representatives or executives of modern democratic governments. In Greece officials were elected annually, and elections were often conducted by poll. The Athenians believed that participation in public affairs was the right and duty of every citizen. (However, they did not regard women and slaves as citizens). Pericles, their greatest orator, speaking on behalf of Athenian democracy in the funeral oration following the war against Sparta in the year 430 B.C., described Athenian democracy as follows:

[Our government] favors the many instead of the few; this is why it is called a democracy. If we look to the laws, they afford equal justice to all in their private differences; if to social standing, advancement in public life falls to reputation for capacity, class considerations not being allowed to interfere with merit; nor again does poverty bar the way; if a man is able to serve the state, he is not hindered by the obscurity of his condition. The freedom which we enjoy in our government extends also to our ordinary life. There, far from exercising a jealous surveillance over each other, we do not feel called upon to be angry with our neighbor for doing what he likes, or even to indulge in those injurious looks which cannot fail to be offensive, although they inflict no positive penalty. But all this ease in our private relations does not make us lawless as citizens. Against this fear is our chief safeguard, teaching us to obey the magistrates and the laws, particularly such as regard the protection of the injured, whether they are actually on the statute book, or belong to that code which, although unwritten, yet cannot be broken without acknowledged disgrace.

Further, we provide plenty of means for the mind to refresh itself from business. We celebrate games and sacrifices all the year round, and the elegance of our private establishments forms a daily source of pleasure and helps to banish the spleen; while the magnitude of our city draws the produce of the world into our harbor, so that to the Athenian the fruits of other countries are as familiar a luxury as those of his own.

. . . We cultivate refinement without extravagance and knowledge without effeminacy; wealth we employ more for use than for show, and place the real disgrace of poverty not in owning to the fact but in declining the struggle against it. Our public men have, besides politics, their private affairs to attend to, and our ordinary citizens, though occupied with the pursuits of industry, are still fair judges of public matters, for, unlike any other nation we regard him who takes no part in these duties not as unambitious but as useless. We Athenians are able to judge at all events if we cannot originate, and instead of looking on discussion as a stumbling-block in the way of action, we think it an indispensable preliminary to any wise action at all.[7]

Athenian democracy, as described by Pericles, continued to grow and develop in various parts of the world after the city's demise. This type of democracy manifested certain principles and a distinctive approach to

7. These extracts, corresponding roughly to the part quoted by the author in Arabic, are quoted here as translated by Joseph Govorse, in *The Complete Writings of Thucydides: The Peloponnesian War* (New York: The Modern Library, 1934), pp. 104–5.

life—recognizing the dignity of man and attempting to manage human affairs in accordance with justice, truth, and popular acceptance. Modern democracy has established certain principles, the most important of which may be summarized as follows:

1. Recognition of basic equality between all individuals.
2. The value of the individual as above that of the state.
3. Government as the servant of the people.
4. The rule of law.
5. Appeal to reason, experiment, and experience.
6. The rule of the majority, with utmost respect for rights of the minority.
7. Democratic method and procedures used to achieve objectives.

Democratic methods and procedures are not an end in themselves, but rather means to an end that lies behind them. The object of democracy is not simply to establish legislative, executive, and judicial organs, since all these are but means to realize the dignity of man. Democracy is not merely a way of government; it is also a way of life. The individual human being is the end, and everything else is a means to that end. The respect and high regard which people have for the democratic approach to government are due to the fact that it is the best approach to achieving the dignity of the individual.

There remain, however, some inadequacies in the present democratic approach, although these are much less pronounced than the deficiencies of Marxism. We leave its detailed examination for our coming book, *Islam is Democratic and Socialist.*

The dignity of man is derived from the fact that he is the most capable of all living things in learning and developing. The value of democracy is that it is the type of government most capable of providing opportunities for man to realize his dignity and honor. In a dictatorship, however, the government denies individuals the right to experiment and assume responsibility, thereby retarding their intellectual, emotional, and moral growth. In contrast to dictatorship, democracy is based on the right to make mistakes. This does not mean that individuals are encouraged to make mistakes for the sake of making mistakes, but rather it is recognition of the fact that freedom requires a choice between various modes of action. Democracy implies learning how to choose, choosing well, and correcting previous mistakes. In fact, all self-discipline and the true exercise of freedom are a series of individual actions in choice and implementation. In other words, freedom of thought, freedom of speech, and freedom of action all require that one accepts responsibility for mistakes in speech and action in accordance with law that is consistent with the constitution.

Democracy is therefore the right to make mistakes, as we learn from the Hadith of the Prophet: "If you do not make mistakes, and then ask for forgiveness, God shall replace you by people who make mistakes, ask for forgiveness, and are forgiven."

Human dignity is so dear to God that individual freedom is not subject to any guardianship, not even that of the Prophet, irrespective of his impeccable morality. God says: "Then remind them, as you are only a reminder. You have no dominion over them." (88:21–22) Reference here is made to the polytheists who refused to worship God and tended the idols, worshipping them and sacrificing to them. Even the Messenger Mohamed, who was not seeking power for himself and whom God described in the Qur'an: "You are of great moral character" (68:4) [was not allowed to have dominion even over such a backward people]. This indicated that no man is perfect enough to be entrusted with the freedom of others, and that the price of freedom is continuous individual vigilance in safeguarding such freedom. In fact, individual freedom is a fundamental right with a corresponding duty, namely, the proper exercise of such freedom.

Since the society of al-mu'minin was incapable of exercising individual freedom in choice and action, the Prophet was appointed as a guardian to prepare them for the responsibility of absolute individual freedom. While exercising such guardianship, he insisted on giving them the right to make mistakes, whenever possible, without subjecting them to undue hardship or difficulty. In that way he was preparing them for democracy, for which they had to be sufficiently mature and intelligent. Such was the order of God when He said: "And it is by the Great Mercy of God that you are kind towards them, and if you had been rough and hard-hearted, they would surely have dispersed from around you. So pardon them and ask forgiveness for them, and consult them; and when you are resolved, then put your trust in God. Surely, God loves those who put their trust [in Him]." (3:159)

This is the verse of Shura [consultation], and consultation, whenever mentioned, whether in this verse or in the following verse—"those who answered the call of their Lord, and perform the prayer, and their affairs are [decided] by Shura [mutual consultation] and pay alms from what We have provided for them" (42:38)—does not refer to democracy. Shura, however, was a necessary stage in preparation for democracy, in due course.

Shura is not an original Islamic precept, but rather a subsidiary one. It is not democracy, but rather the rule of the mature individual who is preparing the nation to become democratic. The original precept of democracy is based on the verse, "Then remind them, as you are only a reminder. You have no dominion over them." (88:21–22)

By the same token, *zakah* is not a socialist practice, it is rather capitalist and is based on the verse, "Take alms out of their wealth, so that you may cleanse them and purify them thereby. And pray for them; your prayer indeed is [a source of] tranquility for them. And God is All-Hearing, All-Knowing." (9:103) Thus, *zakah* is not an original precept of Islam, but rather a subsidiary one. Its purpose is to prepare people psychologically and materially for socialism in due course. The original precept which the verse of *zakah* abrogated is that which reads, "When they ask you what to give away, say all that you do not need" (2:219), as explained above.

The Second Message calls for a return from the subsidiary verses to the original verses, which were temporarily abrogated because of circumstances and material and human limitations. We must now elevate legislation by evolving and basing it on the original Qur'anic verses. In this way we shall welcome the age of socialism and democracy and open the way to absolute individual freedom through worship and humane dealing with other people. This is the Shari'a law of the nation of the Muslims (*muslimin*) that is yet to come, as the earth is now preparing to receive it. It is the duty of the people of the Qur'an [present-day Muslims] to pave the way for *al-muslimin*. And that is the purpose of this book.

SOCIAL EQUALITY: ERASING CLASSES AND DISCRIMINATION

Social equality is the most difficult type of equality to achieve in practice. Since economic and political equality are the preludes to social equality, the latter has not yet been accomplished. It cannot be achieved in the future except through hard work, discipline, education, correction, and change of what is almost natural human behavior. It will represent the peak of civilization, when man moves away from his base animal drives and develops a superior moral character. The law of the jungle—the law of violence and oppressive force—will then be replaced by the law of justice, truth, and compassion—thereby improving the quality of human relations. Consensus will replace force, justice exploitation, freedom oppression, and intelligent community awareness selfish individual drives.

The object of social equality, as in the case of economic equality, is the individual. As stated previously, the individual is the object of all social endeavor, through the means of Islam and the Qur'an. Society is also another method, being the best method yet devised by humanity. The individual who is the object of all means is the individual human being as such. Not even the lowest human being should be made a means to another end. This is why there should be no discrimination on the grounds of birth, race, color, faith, or sex. God says in this connection: "O mankind, We have created you from a male and a female; and We have made you nations and tribes that you may know one another. Verily, the most honorable among you, in the sight of God, is one who is the most righteous among you. Surely, God is All-Knowing, All-Aware." (49:13) The phrase "the most honorable among you, in the sight of God, is one who is the most righteous among you" means that regard is paid to knowledge and moral character. Righteousness is knowledge of God and action in accordance with such knowledge. The phrase "God is All-knowing, All-Aware" means that He acts in accordance with such knowledge. The Prophet said: "All people come from Adam, and Adam is made out of dust. God pays the highest regard to the most righteous."

Absence of social discrimination against the weak and removal of distinctions between individuals and classes are the true signs of civilization. A society which safeguards the rights of the weak, respects their dignity, secures freedom and honor for women, protects children, and is considerate, merciful, and loving to them, is a truly civilized and advanced society.

The family is the first society, and in it the individual learns proper social behavior, respect for law and authority, compassion, forgiveness, and love. The family can best provide education and prepare individuals to be good members of society and of the world at large.

The mother is the foundation of the family; she is the queen of that kingdom. But unfortunately this is not usually recognized. The mother has been, and still is, oppressed; her role in the home has always been, and still is, that of a servant. We believe this has harmful consequences for the upbringing of children and far-reaching, detrimental consequences in the life of society as a whole, at every level.

We have already discussed the question of absolute equality between men and women. But we must emphasise that social equality will not come about spontaneously, as a natural result of progress. It requires planning and the intelligent development of society, through education (ta'lim) and guidance and discipline (tarbiah). Education differs from guidance in that the purpose of education is to enable the individual to gain professional skills suited to his talents and useful to society. Education provides individuals with scientific, technical, administrative, and technological skills, thereby promoting the modernization of society. Education brings specialization and organization, in order to provide for the needs of society. This involves discrimination between men and women, as well as between men and men, so that skills and abilities can be efficiently utilized for the benefit of the community. Such discrimination as occurs in selection of the civil service or administration of society does not necessarily imply social discrimination or inherent superiority of one individual over another.

Accordingly, women and men are recognized as equal even though they may be given different roles in society. Thus, when a woman is being trained to become a mother, her service to the community is not considered less valuable than the service rendered by her brother who is trained to become an engineer, physician, or legislator. There is no limit to training for good motherhood. The more a girl learns, the more valuable she becomes as a mother. It is in the best interests of society that all individuals [men and women] learn some specific task, and preferably one that is both manual and intellectual. That is also in the best interest of the individual himself [or herself], because one's intellectual and moral value does not mature unless he [or she] can perform some type of manual work. God says: "Unto Him ascend the pure words, being elevated by good deeds." (35:10) All these considerations are relevant to the objectives of education.

The objective of guidance and discipline (tarbiah) is to liberate the mind and heart from illusion and falsehood. Through freeing the heart from fear and clarifying thoughts from illusions, one achieves a full and comprehensive intellectual and emotional life which is the object of every living being. Discipline can transform man from savagery to civilization, through refinement of individual habits. Thus, an individual will learn to eat, drink, sleep, sit, speak, and behave in all spheres of his life, public and private, in a civilized fashion, without offending others in any way, manner or fashion. He will try to leave everything in a better state than he found it. Guidance and discipline in all these spheres is learned in schools and clubs, in public places, and even through the media such as radio, television, cinema, theater, the press, books, magazines, lectures, and various types of art. Art forms may be employed to inspire individuals to higher types of behavior.

Society suffers from a state in which most of its members are either adolescents or children, and there are few mature members capable of facing up to the truth. (The tendency of childhood is to play and behave according to the whims and desires of the moment, as well as to escape from anything that may cause failure, pain, or social rejection.) A society characterized by wishful thinking and failure to distinguish between conflicting desires on a rational long-term basis is in need of guidance. Guidance and discipline, in contrast to education, do not emphasize specialization or discrimination between men and women. The need for guidance and discipline is shared by all individuals, including children, limited only by the individuals' ability to receive, assimilate, and implement. We have already discussed the Islamic approach to guidance and discipline and there is no need for repetition here.

Guidance and discipline confront individuals with their responsibility and assist them to shoulder such responsibility in order to become mature individuals. The difference between children and adolescents on the one hand, and [mature] men and women on the other, is that men and women act freely and accept responsibility for their action, while adolescents and children either refuse to act in fear of the consequent responsibility, or act and try to evade and escape responsibility for their action.

Conclusion

In conclusion, we repeat that religion has a pyramid shape, the peak being with God at infinity, and the base with humanity: "Religion with God is Islam." (6:19) In the past religion has been lowered from its peak down to the level of human needs and capabilities, in the form of Shari'a. The peak of the pyramid will remain forever beyond our reach. As individuals, each one will continue to develop in his understanding of religion, through knowledge of the material world and of ourselves. God says: "We shall show them Our signs in the material world and within themselves, until it becomes manifest to them that He is the Truth. Is your Lord not sufficient witness upon everything?" (41:53) He also says: "They learn nothing of His knowledge except what He wishes them to learn." (2:255) God wishes us to have more of His knowledge every moment. He says: "Everyday He [reveals Himself] in a fresh state." (55:29) In other words, He is always revealing Himself to His creation so that they may know Him. He is the one who is teaching us. He says: "And make no haste to recite the Qur'an before its revelation is completed unto you, but only say, Lord, bestow on me increase of knowledge." (20:114) Such additional knowledge is in fact higher ascent from the base of the pyramid of Islam to its peak in continuous evolution. As man develops in understanding of religion, he evolves his Shari'a in accordance with his needs and capabilities, which are increasingly refined and purified.

Individuals progress in understanding religion, thereby proceeding to *Shari'a fardiyah*, their individual law, while societies develop as a result of individual development, and their Shari'a also becomes more refined and humane. This reflects a movement up the ladder of the pyramid whose base is the Shari'a of the First Message.

If the peak of Islam with respect to property is the verse "When they ask you what to give away, say all that you do not need" (2:219), then its base is the verse "Take alms out of their wealth, so that you may cleanse them and purify them thereby. And pray for them; your prayer indeed is [a source of] tranquility for them." (9:103) This illustrates the difference between the First Message and Second Message with respect to property. The First Message conceded private ownership and payment of the specified annual sum [of *zakah*], since people were incapable of a superior standard. Achieving a higher level of conduct was left to individual endeavor, each according to individual capability. Encouragement for further moral growth came in the Hadith "others have a right to your property besides *zakah.*" The verse which says "Say: if you love God, then follow me, and God will love you" (3:31) reflects the Prophet's own Shari'a with respect to property, and as a matter of worship, which is closer to the peak of Islam.

The peak of religion with respect to politics is illustrated by the verses: "Then remind them, as you are only a reminder. You have no dominion over them" (88:21–22), while the verse of *Shura* is closer to its base. It reads: "And it is by the Great Mercy of God that you are kind towards them, and if you had been rough and hard-hearted, they would surely have dispersed from around you. So pardon them and ask forgiveness for them, and consult them, and when you are resolved, then put your trust in God. Surely, God loves those who put their trust [in Him]." (3:159) Another verse which represents the First Message is, "And when the forbidden months have passed, slay the idolaters wherever you find them and take them [captive], and beleaguer them, and lie in wait for them at every place of ambush. But if they repent and observe prayer and pay *zakah*, then leave their way [free]. Surely God is Most Forgiving, Merciful." (9:5) This was the basis for the Shari'a of *jihad*, while the verse of *Shura* [consultation] provided the Shari'a of government, in accordance with the principle of guardianship of the mature individual [the Prophet] over the community.

Although the First Message was not democratic, it approached democracy at a time when society as a whole was not yet ready for true democracy.

Again, the First Message, while not socialist, was close to socialism at a time when society was not ready for real scientific socialism.

Since humanity has evolved over fourteen centuries [since the time of the First Message] towards maturity, becoming, through the grace of God, materially and intellectually capable of implementing both socialism and democracy, Islam must be propagated in these terms. This signifies a development from the more primitive base of the Shari'a of the First Message to a less primitive level, somewhat approaching the peak, while the peak remains, as always, in the realm of ultimate individuality. The beginning of the new Islamic base is the threshold of socialism, by prohibiting the ownership of the means and sources of production by a single individual or a few persons in association. This opens the gates of Islamic legislation into socialism.

The beginning of the new Islamic base is the threshold of democracy. Here the right to vote is secured to every citizen of a certain age, male or female, as is the right to nominate oneself for election. This opens the gates of Islamic legislation into democracy.

This process is called *tatwir al-tashri'* [evolution of the law], which signifies development from a subsidiary Qur'anic text to an original text. It is a shift from one text of the Qur'an to another.

There is an area of overlap between the First Message and the Second Message, such as the *Shariaht al-'ibadat* [worship practices], in which there is no evolution except where it opens into the realm of *Shari'a fardiyah*, law of the individual. Each individual may grow through the grace of God and by perfecting imitation [of the Prophet] until he finally achieves his own individuality which distinguishes him from other members of the human herd.

Shari'a fardiyah, individual law rather than community law, is the original principle of Islam, just as the individual rather than the community is Islam's original goal. But people have grown so accustomed to living in communities that they become bewildered and frightened when one speaks to them about *Shari'a fardiyah*. Moreover, *Shari'a fardiyah* addresses a stage of maturity and responsibility, whereas most people remain irresponsible children who wish others to shoulder their responsibilities. Generally, when responsibility is assumed, it is done as part of the herd, and along the well-trodden path. The self shrinks from accepting responsibility and from starting out on an unknown path.

The threshold of the Second Message is the First Message, except those aspects of its Shari'a that are subject to evolution. There is no evolution of *al-'ibadat* [worship practices], except the *zakah*, alms in accordance with the specified proportions, which was previously made one of the pillars of the faith only because the people were incapable of anything better. Otherwise, the real pillar of the faith is *zakah* according to the standard of the Prophet, because it is an original principle based on firm primary sources of religion. There will be evolution, however, in the realm of *al-mu'amalat* [the rules of social transactions]. These include the fundamental individual rights, and economic and political structures. All matters associated with social change must evolve with society and exhibit the necessary vitality for growth and renewal.

The original principles of the Second Message are vitality, development, and renewal. The diligent worshipper [*al-salik*] who is evolving with the Second Message must seek to renew his intellectual and emotional life at every moment of the day and night. His ideal is God, who describes Himself as "Every day He [reveals Himself] in a fresh state" (55:29), and yet "nothing distracts Him from anything else." At the beginning, one professes the faith, "*la ilah ila-Allah* and Mohamed is the Messenger of God," and endeavors, through imitation of the Prophet, to achieve certainty in that "*la ilah ila-Allah.*"[1] Further perfection in imitation of the Prophet leads one to realize that ultimately faith is only fully professed by the object of such profession [God] in accordance with the verse, "God bears witness [and maintains], and so do the angels and the knowledgeable ones, that there is no god other than God Himself. He is Fair, Self-Sufficient, and Wise." (3:18) At this point the individual enters upon the threshhold of servitude to and direct audience with God, without any intermediary, and he is told, "Say God and leave them to their futile play." (6:91) The phrase "say God" implies "being" God [in the sense of acquiring a progressive degree of His qualities]. This is the sphere of *Shari'a fardiyah,* law of the individual.

When one thus ascends the ladder of the Second Message, past the threshhold of the First Message, he would have thereby covered the seven steps of the ladder: from *al-islam* to *al-'iman, al-ihsan, 'ilm al-yaqin, 'ayn al-yaqin, haqq al-yaqin,* into *al-islam* once more. Then he starts afresh on a new level into a new cycle, and so on, indefinitely.

Islam is a spiral, having its beginning with us in the law of the community and its end is with God in infinity. Anyone ascending this ladder continues towards God in infinitude. Thus, every moment, he gains increased knowledge and consequently surrenders himself, more and more, to God. All this would renew his intellectual and emotional life. Entrance to the level of *Shari'a fardiyah,* in pursuit of this process, is imperative and not difficult to attain. The real test of perfection, however, which is extremely difficult to satisfy, is to have your truth with God and to render your *Shari'a fardiyah* an integral aspect of that truth. This state,

1. Professing that Mohamed is the Messenger of God and imitating him is a means to the object of realizing, with certainty, that *la ilah ila-Allah,* that is, God is the only true God and the only Actor in the world.

however, is impossible for any human individual to achieve completely, since it is an infinite and never-ending process.

This is not idealistic talk, because it has a practical beginning that is placed firmly on the ground in order to lead everyone upwards in *itlaq*, infinitude, at varying degrees of achievement, each according to his level of knowledge. Everybody is ascending this ladder; "Above every knowledgeable one is another who is even more knowledgeable" (12:76), until knowledge itself culminates with [God] the "Knowledgeable of all the unknown." (9:78)

This means there is no limit to the perfection man can achieve, not ever. Man's destiny is to rise to the level of his Lord, and the means for achieving this is realistically based on worship practice and social relations with others—*'ibadah* and *mu'amalah*, as explained above. It is enough for man that God desires from him such perfection as no eye has ever seen, and no ear has ever heard, and has never occurred to any human being.

To You, my Lord, I give as many thanks as You are worthy.

Glossary of Selected Terms

al-dhat: The Divine Being
al-dhikr: Remembrance through worship
al-haq: Truth as opposed to *batil* or falsehood
(al)-'aqidah: Dogma or belief
al-salik: The diligent intelligent worshiper
(al)-takhir: Freedom of choice and will

batin: Hidden or deeper meaning

fardiyah: Singularity

hadd (pl. *hudod*): Specified penalty for the particular offenses named in the
    Qur'an
Hadith: Statement of the Prophet
al-haqiqa: Ultimate truth or knowledge
hukm al-waqt: The dictates of the time

'ibadat: Worship practices
Iblis (pl. *abalisa*): Satan, devils
itlaq: Infinitude or infinity

la ilah ila-Allah: There is no god but God

mu'amalat: Social transactions or dealings
al-mu'awadah: Reciprocity
mukhayr: Enjoying freedom of choice or will
mu'minin (singular *mu'min*): Believers even at superficial level

muslimin (singular *muslim*): True submitters and surrenderers of individual will to
    God
musayr: Manipulated to predetermined destiny

(al)-qasas: Retribution
Shari'a fardiyah: Individual law or code of conduct
Sunnah: The Prophet's conduct and statements

(al)-tariqah: Emphasized methodology
(al) tasir: Manipulation to predetermined destiny
tawhid: Monotheism. Living in accordance with the belief that there is no god
    but God
thuna'yah: Duality

wahdat al-fa'il: Unity of the actor. That God is the only true actor and His Will
    the only effective will
zahir: Ostensible or apparent meaning

Index

Abdu, Mohamed: 21

Absolute: *see* Infinitude

Abraham, Prophet: 57–58, 85, 115, 116, 120, 151–52

Abrogation *(Naskh)*: Adam's freedom and, 103; of divorce, 143; human sacrifice, 57; of Qur'anic texts, 21, 24, 37, 88, 126, 134, 161

Abu al-'La' al Ma'rri (poet): 66

Abu al-Qasim al-Jinayd (sufi): 73, 95

Abu Bakr: 20, 138n14, 150

Adam and Eve: 33, 142, 144; creation of, 96–99; foregiveness for, 99–104

'Adl, al- (justice): 77, 92, 133

Afghany, Jamal al-Din al-: 21

Ahl al-Kitab (People of the Book): 19–20, 22, 72, 76, 115–16

Ahmad, Prophet (Prophet Mohamed): 120

Aisha (Prophet's wife): 51

Aman (safe conduct): 22

'Amru ibn al-'As (conqueror of Egypt): 58–59

Angels: Adam and, 103; humans and, 106

'Aqidah, al-: *see* Dogma

Apostasy: Ustadh Mahmoud accused of, 15; wars of, 138n14

Arab Human Rights Day: 26

Arabic: alphabetical letters in Qur'an, 125–29; language of the Qur'an, 29, 33, 149

Ash'ariun, al- (Arabian tribe): 156

Asma (elder daughter of Ustadh Mahmoud): 17

Batin (hidden meaning): 87–88, 94, 97–98; Second Message and, 147, 149

Believers: *see* Mu'minin

Brothers: as nation of *Muslimin*, 36, 150

Capitalism: 52–54, 138, 153

Christ: *see* Jesus

Christians: 19, 22, 61, 117–18, 120–22, 131–32

Circumcision, female: *see* Pharaonic circumcision

Civilization: evolution of, 49–51, 150, 161–64, Western, 52–55, 59, 61

Communism: 53–55, 59, 61, 154–57

Community: freedom in, 63–64, 68, 132–33; relationship to individual, 56–61, 63, 73, 82, 152; Legislative Decree and, 92

Companions of the Prophet *(sahabah)*: 20; nation of *Mu'minin* and, 150; rationalists and, 85

Conscience: hidden, 68, 71; purity of, 72

173

Human rights: 26–28

Humanity: creation of, 80–81; dignity of, 159–60; evolution of, 50, 59–61, 75, 77–79, 84, 98–100, 165–69

Hypocrites: in Islam, 124, 126

'Ibadat (worship practices): 63, 68, 123, 167, 169

Iblis (Satan): 33, 50, 96–100

Ibn al-Farid (sufi): 93

Ibn Taymiya: 21

Ihsan, al-: see Good

Ijtihad (creative juristic reasoning): 22–23

Iman, al- (true belief): stage of al-islam, 44–46, 124–25, 130–32, 136, 147, 152

Imitation: human faculty of, 127; of Prophet Mohamed, 166–68

Individual: goal of Islam, 62–63, 132, 152, 165–69; freedom and, 51–52, 64, 66–74, 84–85, 110–11, 132, 152, 159–60, 162; relationship to community, 56–58, 68, 73; relationship to universe, 59–61

Infinitude (itlaq): determinism and, 104–5; God and, 33, 52, 108, 114, 147–49, 168–69; Islam and, 64–65

Intelligence: definition of, 83

Islam: civilization and, 49, 150–51; essence of, 32–35, 37, 75, 113, 115, 148; freedom and, 63–64, 112; levels of, 44–47, 137; messages of, 31, 122–23, 146–47; original precepts in, 132–45; submission to, 38, 113–15; trinity of, 118–22. See also Constitution

Islam, al-: intellectual spiral of, 44–45, 124–25, 130–31, 136–37, 148, 168

Islamic jurisprudence (usul al-fiqh): 6; evolution of, 20–21, 23–24

Islamic Trinity: 118–22

Islamization: of Sudan, 9–13

Itlaq: see Infinitude

Jesus: 42, 57, 116, 118, 120–21, 131

Jews: 19, 22, 69, 118, 120–21, 131–32

Jihad: 126, 132–34, 166; major, 131, 135

Jinn (spirits): 110, 133

Jiziah (personal tax): 11, 22, 137

Justice, Divine: 86; see also 'Adl, al-

Khalwah (religious seclusion): 4

Khidr (insight of the heart): 95

Knowledge: God and, 36, 41–42, 63, 99, 130–31; realm of, 93, 169

La ilah ila-Allah (there is no god but God): 36, 38, 116, 125, 168

Legislation: Islamic, 37, 68, 70, 72, 153

Legislative Decree: 91–92, 99, 101, 117

Love: 77; will and, 112

Luqman (God's true slave): 131

Mahmoud, Mustafa (Egyptian author): 24

Mahmoud, Ustadh (Mahmoud Mohamed Taha): fundamentalist opposition to, 8; life and death of, 2–19, 25–26; publication of leaflet, 10–14; Rufa'h incident, 3–4; vision of Islam, 5, 10–14, 18–28

Mahr (bride-price): 6–7

Man: God's viceregent, 111–12; see also Humanity

Marriage: divorce and, 142–43; polygamy and, 140; Republicans and, 6–7; Shari'a law of, 22, 38; society and, 153

Marxism: ideology of, 53, 154–56

Materialism: progress and, 51–55; spiritualism vs., 78–79, 150–51

Mecca: 19; first stage of revelation in, 21, 37, 125–26, 130

Medina: 19; second stage of revelation in, 21, 37, 125–26

Messengers: God's sending of, 82, 108; and prophethood, 41; of Second Message, 42

Mind: control of, 74; development of, 75, 79, 83, 94–95, 100–101, 129; illusion and, 87–88

Mohamed, Prophet: life of, 19–20; as perfect model, 19, 34n4, 35, 37, 44, 52,

Second Message of Islam: audience for, 21, 27, 36, 43, 46, 165–69; Qur'an and, 146–47, 161; Ustadh Mahmoud's proclamation of, 4–5, 23–25, 37. *See also* Abrogation, Postponement, Revelation

Self: attainment of superior, 66, 71, 107; control of, 131, 135; God and, 94; prohibitions on, 70, 101–2; unity of, 109, 114; will and, 83, 101

Shari'a (historical Islamic law): development of, 20–24, 38–41, 76–77, 108–9, 134–35, 137, 141, 161, 165–69; discrimination in, 22; Qur'an and, 87; religion and, 33–34; Sudanese law and, 6–16, 24–27; Sunnah and, 35. *See also* Haqiqah, Mu'amalat, Shari'a fardiyah

Shari'a fardiyah (individual law): 68, 75, 92–93, 95, 110; ultimate Islam and, 152, 165–68. *See also 'Ibadat*

Shi'a sect: 20

Shura: see Consultation

Sin: 68, 71, 86, 90–92; consequence of, 144

Sir al-sir (secret of the conscience): 71, 129, 131

Slave: God and, 65, 93, 109–10, 135, 137–38, 147; Luqman, 131

Slavery: society and, 137–38

Socialism: achievement of, 54, 153–57, 167

Society: needs of modern, 53, development of, 57, 75, 82; good, 152–53, 161–64

Spirit: will and, 80, 83, 101

Submission: Adam and, 99; God's Will and, 18–19, 34, 38, 45–47, 105; Islam and, 113; meaning of, 114–15

Successors of the Companions of the Prophet *(tab'in):* 20

Sudan: establishment of republic of, 2–3; courts of, 6, 14–18; non-Muslims in, 25–27; penal code of, 3, 12–13

Sufis (mystics): 5n5; 71, 73, 86, 88, 93, 108, 156

Sufur, al- (modest dress): 143–45

Sunnah (tradition of the Prophet): basis for Second Message, 5, 11, 34–35; expression of morality, 52

Supreme Being: *see Dhat, al-*

Surrender: *see* Submission to God

Tabari, al-: 20

Tab'in: see Successors of the Companions of the Prophet

Tahkim (arbitration): 6

Takhir: see Free Will

Ta'lim (education): 163–64

Tarbiah (discipline): 163–64

Tariqa (methodology): 35, 40–41, 44; *see also* Sunnah

Tasir, al-: see Determinism

Tawhid: see Monotheism

Ta'zir (discretionary punishment): 11

Time *(bi-qadar):* 92–93, 108

Time, dicates of: *see Hukm al-waqt*

Torah: 102, 118–21

Trinity, Islamic: 118–23

Truth: See *Haqiqah*

'Umar ibn al-Khatab: 45, 58–59

Unity *(fardyah):* 91, 93, 95, 110, 152

Unity of the Actor *(wahdat al-fa'il):* 89, 95

Universe: creation of, 80, 100; relationship to individual, 59–61, 77–79

Usul al-fiqh: see Islamic jurisprudence

Will: God's, 76, 80–81, 83–84, 91, 100–101, 104; love and, 112; submission to God's, 114–15

Women: chastity of, 143–45; discrimination against, 22–23, 62, 163; equality for, 62, 139–42; Republicans and, 5–7, 25; segregation of, 145

Worship: object of, 109–10; practices *('ibadat),* 63, 68, 123; submission in, 115

Worshiper, diligent *(al-salik):* 45, 88, 95, 130, 168

THE SECOND MESSAGE OF ISLAM

was composed in 10-point Goudy Old Style and leaded 2 points on a Linotron 202
by Coghill Book Typesetting Company;
with display type set in Nicolini Broadpen by Arnold & Debel Inc., Typographers;
and ornaments provided by Jōb Litho Services;
printed by sheet-fed offset on 55-pound, acid-free Glatfelter Antique Cream,
Smyth-sewn and bound over binder's boards in Joanna Arrestox B,
by Maple-Vail Book Manufacturing Group, Inc.;
with dust jackets printed in one color by Niles & Phipps Lithographers
and published by

SYRACUSE UNIVERSITY PRESS
Syracuse, New York 13244-5160